Exiled Emissary: George H. Earle III
Soldier, Sailor, Diplomat, Governor, Spy

Christopher J. Farrell

Exiled Emissary: George H. Earle III
Soldier, Sailor, Diplomat, Governor, Spy

Christopher J. Farrell

Academica Press
Washington~London

Library of Congress Cataloging-in-Publication Data

Names: Farrell, Christopher J. (author)
Title: Exiled emissary : george h. earle III, soldier, sailor, diplomat, governor, spy | Christopher J. Farrell
Description: Washington : Academica Press, 2021. | Includes references.
Identifiers: LCCN 2021933344 | ISBN 9781680538861 (hardcover) | 9781680538878 (paperback) 9781680538885 (e-book)

Dedication

For Shea
The inspiration, the faith, and the future.

Contents

Jan 1943

Germany Surrenders to Russians in Stalingrad, Feb 1943

FDR dies April 1945

List of Illustrations

Acknowledgments

My grandmother, Helen FitzGerald, inspired this book in the summer of 1967. She first told me, as a young boy, about how my grandfather, Jack FitzGerald, had worked with Governor George Earle to help Jewish businessmen and their families escape from Nazi Germany in 1936. Jack FitzGerald was a founding member of the New York Coffee & Sugar Exchange, and a commodities broker. George H. Earle III was the president of Flamingo Sugar Mills in Philadelphia, Pennsylvania and Jack's client, business partner and close friend.

Decades later, I have had the great privilege of telling the story of a remarkable man of character and conviction. Research was an on-again, off-again project that spanned many years. It included trips to the National Archives and in-person talks with George Earle's son, Lawrence, as well as other Earle family members.

The manuscript was written between May and November 2020. I wrote it with the encouragement of Dr. Shea Bradley Garrison, PhD. I had told Shea of my boyhood memories, and my years of research. She found the George Earle story fascinating and compelling – urging me to pick-up where I had left off and get to work writing. I am deeply indebted to Shea for the inspiration to write, the faith in me and the Earle story, and her unwavering support, insightful advice and steadfast devotion. Without Shea there would be no book.

I have several other people to thank for their time, information, encouragement, suggestions and assistance: Melanie

Earle Lynagh & family; Jackie Earle-Cruickshank; Edward Wharton Shober; Christopher and Rachel Titus; COL Randy Williams, USA (Ret.); John J. Dziak, PhD; David Thomas, PhD; Diana West; and Juliana Geran Pilon, PhD.

We are all indebted to the work and memory of M. Stanton Evans (*Stalin's Secret Agents: The Subversion of Roosevelt's Government*) for his nearly exhaustive treatment detailing Soviet penetration of the Franklin Delano Roosevelt's administration. Evans names and backs it all up with scrupulous research. We now know the agents, fellow travelers, cooperators, sympathizers, and dupes: Alger Hiss; Harry Dexter White; Harry Hopkins; Henry Wallace; Lauchlin Currie; Owen Lattimore; David Niles; and Henry Morgenthau, among many others – known and still unknown.

Likewise, we have the thoughtful, penetrating analysis of Diana West (*American Betrayal: The Secret Assault on Our Nation's Character*) that ties the strands of what she calls the "Lost Narrative" of history together in a way that fills in many historical blanks and gaps, whether deliberately air-brushed from the homogenized "Court histories," or simply overlooked. Her treatment of Earle, Roosevelt, the peace initiative, and the Katyn Forest Massacre are essential reading.

I am grateful to serve as the channel for this important chapter of overlooked history.

> Then I heard the voice of the Lord, saying, 'Whom shall
> I send, and who will go for Us?' Then I said, 'Here am I.
> Send me!'
> – Isaiah 6:8

Foreword

John J. Dziak, PhD

The Roosevelt era of the New Deal and World War II may appear to be an artifact of history to many, but it emits a resonance well into the 21st Century. Like a specter its effects still dwell in our culture, politics, diplomacy, and intelligence history, often in ways unforeseen. One of these unforeseen ways is the appearance of Christopher Farrell's book, *Exiled Emissary: George H. Earle III – Soldier, Sailor Diplomat, Governor, Spy*, a fast moving and revelatory account of an accomplished politician, polymath, and successful businessman who served President Franklin D. Roosevelt during the years of the New Deal and the Second World War.

A man of strong conviction and independent spirit, Earle served with distinction as a naval officer in World War I. He received the Navy Cross for his actions while commanding a motor patrol boat disabled by an internal explosion and fire. This experience, his energy, and his years in business and politics helped to propel him (despite his Republican pedigree) into serving the Roosevelt administration as a diplomat in the 1930s, and Assistant Naval Attaché in Turkey during World War II.

This latter part of his service to FDR is especially riveting because of its intelligence dimensions, both at the time of Earle's service and in the post-World War II years. In accounts of Earle and of that period, these intelligence dimensions weren't that manifest; their opacity being driven by the very nature of the intelligence craft and generally hidden or ignored Soviet subversive operations, well before the advent of the Cold War. But Earle, possessed of a natural spirit, saw through the maze of bureaucratic and diplomatic doubletalk, and focused in on the hidden potentialities for US national interests -- that got him on the wrong side of high politics, both foreign and US.

It took a former professional US intelligence officer, Christopher Farrell, to winkle out the obscure and connective threads of the intelligence games, subversion, arcane diplomacy, and lost opportunities that Earle both witnessed and partook thereof during World War II, and in the controversies of the post-war period.[i] Farrell, possessed of access to Earle's papers, but also an astute student of Twentieth Century totalitarian history and associated intelligence, and counterintelligence operations, pulled Earle's story together in a way that sheds different light on several events whose implications still live with us. Without repeating Farrell's superb narrative, it is worth mentioning several of these to get a sense of Earle's instincts for strategic moments in statecraft and their intelligence connections.

Earle had strong faith in FDR and basically served as FDR's personal emissary, despite his lower-level Assistant Naval Attaché status in Turkey, a status that functioned as a useful cover. Earle could communicate directly with the President but, as events revealed, that was done through Harry Hopkins, FDR's close advisor and confidante. It turns out that given Hopkin's pro-Soviet attitude and the deep controversies surrounding his probable relationship to Soviet intelligence, Earle found that his communications to FDR were not registering the way he had hoped. And it wasn't only Hopkins. Roosevelt was surrounded by Soviet

---

[i] In this particular regard, Christopher Farrell was ably preceded by Diana West in her book *American Betrayal: The Secret Assault on Our Nation's Character* (NY: St. Martin's Press: 2013). While her coverage of George H. Earle III is not the focus of her book, she captures Earle's frustrated efforts to warn FDR about both the Soviet Katyn massacres, and the German military's approaches to the US and UK for a separate peace – which were dismissed by FDR and his pro-Soviet advisors, and by the UK. Farrell provides all the grim details in his exhaustive work.

sympathizers and agents of influence who exercised far greater influence with FDR than an outsider like Earle. On top of that, FDR was not at all sympathetic to data, assessments, and intelligence that pointed to Stalin's massacres, his other crimes, and his intelligence operations against the US both before and during World War II. Christopher Farrell's broad-ranging narrative lays this all out in compelling detail.

But Earle also had to contend with other powerful interests, not just those of FDR and his entourage. He stepped on the turf not only of a State Department that resented Earle's thrusts into matters it considered its territory, but he also incurred unwanted attention from MI6, the UK foreign intelligence service, over his contacts with the anti-Hitler German military conspirators whose soundings for taking out Hitler followed by a negotiated peace might have endangered the Allied unconditional surrender demand. Such a move was also anathema to Stalin and his secret police. Earle even suspected an assassination attempt on him in Turkey, masked as an automobile accident, instigated possibly by an MI6 official.

Earle discovered that his interpretation of his mission certainly was not that of FDR. His discovery of the truth of the culpability of Stalin and the Soviet secret police, the NKVD, in the mass murder of Polish officers in the Katyn forest and his warnings of coming Soviet aggression and their post-War plans, incensed not only the Soviets, but FDR as well. When Earle continued to press the issue, in March 1945, he was ordered by the President to shut up—following which Earle was exiled to Samoa to an inferior position apparently designed to punish him for truth-telling. Roosevelt died in April 1945 and George Earle arranged his way back to the US by the following July. During the early post-War period he continued the fight to signal the dangers of an aggressive USSR, including testimony before Congress.

In summary, *Exiled Emissary* offers a number of embedded but unspoken insights and lessons on the crafts of Intelligence and counterintelligence, not surprising coming from an author seasoned in the counterintelligence craft and the arts of investigation in his current professional position.

Here are just a few of those insights and lessons one may elicit from Farrell's narrative that caught this writer's attention:

- In the argot of intelligence, George H. Earle III was a "singleton" operative, but not a member of an institutionalized intelligence service unless we count his time as Assistant Naval Attaché, a preserve of the Office of Naval Intelligence (ONI). Yet, he operated as an asset of FDR himself, reporting to FDR, an unorthodox arrangement in the intelligence business, then or now. His attaché designation appeared to be a cover, masking his one-man, Presidential-authorized intelligence operations while in Turkey. Turkey was an attractive intelligence listening post for Nazi Germany, Japan, the US, its Western Allies and, of course, the USSR. Think West Berlin or Vienna following World War II.

- Despite his shabby treatment at the hands of FDR and his leftist advisors, Earle remained loyal and professionally deferential to his Commander-in-Chief -- an unrequited loyalty as it turned out. But that loyalty didn't degrade his grasp of reality and unpleasant truths. A natural intelligencer, Earle appeared quickly to sense the hidden agendas and drivers of statecraft, especially in their intelligence dimensions and strategic implications.

- George Earle, probably unwittingly at first, stumbled into the reality of Soviet penetration of the highest levels of the US government and the roles of Agents-of-Influence whose tasks stretched far beyond *mere* espionage and into the realms of policy influence, manipulation, deception and, in the idiom of 21st Century political warfare, active measures and information operations. Were Earle observing the 2021 scene today, would he recognize the old Soviet penetration ethos being reprised in neo-Marxist utopian schemas and the massive penetration, intelligence, and influence operations of the Peoples' Republic of China, not only in the US but world-wide as well?

Given what Christopher Farrell has mapped for us in *Exiled Emissary*, Earle likely would have smoked out those unpleasant realities immediately.

♦

John J. Dziak, Ph.D. is a former senior intelligence officer and executive in the Office of the Secretary of Defense and the Defense Intelligence Agency, and author of the award-winning *Chekisty: A History of the KGB*.

Introduction:

A Man of His Convictions

It is dangerous to be right when the government is wrong.
— Voltaire

George Howard Earle III was a man of his convictions. Earle's convictions would catapult him to the heights of American political power, international diplomacy, and wartime intrigue. Earle made large financial contributions to FDR, and even stepped aside from the 1940 Democratic nomination for the presidency in order for FDR to make an unprecedented run for a third term. Earle admired his friend and political ally, but he was not afraid of FDR. Earle told FDR the truth when the president did not want to hear it. Earle carried a message that may have ended World War II in 1943. He also exposed an "ally" as a brutal, murderous, lying, totalitarian regime.

"True believers," even sophisticated ones, can have a very hard time of it. To say what one means and mean what one says — especially to those persons in whom one trusts and believes — is an act of personal conviction that is quite rare. It is more than a leap of faith. It is an act of trust. It is courageous.

Fear, insecurity, and cynicism have a way of hollowing out one's convictions. They are the termites that eat at the foundations of what we would like to believe are our principles and values. Our convictions are that short list of things that are of utmost importance to us — that in the parlance of Plutarch's *Life of Brutus* — one is willing to "fall on one's sword over." Men of conviction, such as

George H. Earle III, are rare. Sadly, we are too often more familiar with the compromisers and the double-talkers who spend their time checking the political winds and hedging their bets.

George Earle, the great-great-grandnephew of Benjamin Franklin, and related to a string of other prominent early colonists and founding Americans, was not afraid to break conventions, try new endeavors and speak his mind. Lawrence W. Earle, George Earle's 93-year-old son, explained his father in crystal clear terms during an interview in December 2016: "He would do any damn thing he felt like!"

Those convictions would result in Earle's banishment — an exile to Samoa imposed by FDR. Earle's initiative, drive and savvy made the establishment nervous and drove some within the FDR White House to open a secret investigation of Earle's activities in Istanbul. The power establishment of Washington, DC was leery of George Earle because he did not need them. He was not for sale and he was not in need of a government title to know who he was.

Chris Farrell

Washington, DC

November 2020

Chapter 1

Earle and FDR

Millions of American men and women would gladly have
given their lives if it meant ending World War II a day
sooner than it did. I believe one man had a chance to
shorten the conflict by more than 18 months – and
brushed it off. His name? President Franklin D.
Roosevelt.[1]

George H. Earle III
Former Governor of Pennsylvania,
U.S. Minister to Austria and Bulgaria
Assistant U.S. Naval Attaché, Istanbul
Philadelphia, PA
July 1958

◆

… I specifically forbid you to publish any information or
opinion about an ally that you have acquired while in
office or in the service of the United States Navy. In view
of your wish for continued active service, I shall withdraw
any previous understanding that you are serving as an
emissary of mine and I shall direct the Navy Department
to continue your employment wherever they can make use
of your services.[2]

Letter from President Franklin D. Roosevelt to
Commander George H. Earle III, U.S.N.R.
March 24, 1945

◆

George H. Earle III told President Franklin D. Roosevelt two things FDR simply did not wish to hear:

> 1. In January 1943, German intelligence, diplomatic and military leaders offered to turn over Adolf Hitler and his inner circle, dead or alive, to the Allies under terms of an Armistice, and an agreement for a subsequent attack on the Soviet forces moving west through Central Europe; and

> 2. The Katyn Forest Massacres in April and May 1940 – wherein more than 22,000 Polish military officers, government officials, academics, business owners, lawyers, priests, and others ("decapitating" Polish society) – was carried out by the Soviet NKVD ("People's Commissariat for Internal Affairs," the Soviet secret police) over claims the Nazis had murdered the victims in 1941.

As to the first point, FDR's response to Earle was silence. Since January 1943, Earle served as the "Assistant U.S. Naval Attaché" in Istanbul, Turkey as FDR's personal emissary to the Balkans – thin diplomatic cover for Earle's activities in a wartime neutral city renown for intrigue, espionage, and the occasional body found floating in the Bosporus. Months passed following Earle's stunning message conveying the proposal from the German resistance ("*Widerstand*" in German). Earle sent follow up dispatches via diplomatic pouch to FDR, and had clandestine meetings with German resistance leaders who articulated detailed plans for the neutralization of Hitler, installation of an interim German government, and the means of establishing contact with Allied armies for an immediate armistice on the Western Front. Eventually, Earle got his answer from FDR: "All such applications for a negotiated peace should be referred to the Supreme Allied Commander, General Eisenhower."

Earle memorialized his reaction to FDR's reply: "In diplomatic language, this was the final runaround. Even if we did get to Eisenhower, the matter would be referred back to Roosevelt for a final decision. The President's answer was therefore a clear indication of his complete disinterest in this plan to end the war."[3]

The German resistance, stunned by Roosevelt's rejection and demand for "unconditional surrender," took the decision to move on to the last-ditch July 1944 bomb plot, known as Operation Valkyrie, executed by Colonel Claus Graf von Stauffenberg at Hitler's *Wolfsschanze* (Wolf's Lair) headquarters in East Prussia. The assassination attempt failed and much of the German resistance leadership was arrested and executed.

Concerning Earle's Katyn Forest Massacre investigation and findings – that the Soviet NKVD had brutally slaughtered the cream of Polish society – FDR rejected the autopsy reports, interviews, sworn affidavits and other evidence Earle compiled from the International Committee of the Red Cross, neutral observers, and Earle's own network of Central European agents. FDR insisted that Earle's evidence was merely German propaganda. "George," said Roosevelt, "the Germans could have rigged things up." FDR ordered Earle's report suppressed.[4]

Earle was vindicated in 1989, fifteen years after his death, when the Russian government officially acknowledged and condemned the perpetration of the Katyn Forest Massacres by the NKVD, as well as the subsequent cover-up by the Soviet government.[5]

Earle defined his understanding of the real threat to Western Civilization posed by Soviet Communism in classified "Eyes Only" cables to the President since April 1944. As presidential emissary to the Balkans, Earle had interviewed hundreds of Soviet refugees and developed his own source network that reported on the depravity of the Red Army as it rolled west.

In May 1944 and March 1945, Earle and FDR had heated exchanges in the White House over the threats posed by the Soviet Union in post-war Europe. After the March 1945 White House meeting, Earle notified FDR of his intention to publish his findings concerning the Katyn Forest Massacre and the looming Soviet threat to western democracy. FDR forbade Earle to publish any such information or opinion, withdrew Earle's status as presidential emissary and exiled the former Pennsylvania governor, ambassador, and attaché to be deputy military governor of Samoa.

The exile of a presidential emissary, more than 7,000 miles from Washington, DC, illuminates the character of both FDR and Earle. It is the difference between a political ideologue, blinded to one course of action at any and all costs, and a man of conviction sounding the clarion call with a clear vision of the impending Soviet threat that would freeze the world into a half-century long Cold War that cost the world thousands of lives and millions of persons' political imprisonment. Within four months of the shameful banishment to Samoa, FDR was dead, and President Truman would recall Earle home to the United States.

As we shall see, newly declassified "Top Secret" records unearthed from government archives will provide new context for evaluating the amazing career and predictive analysis of George H. Earle III, and raise compelling questions and fresh answers concerning:

- How World War II might have ended 18-months earlier;

- The Soviet intelligence penetration of the FDR White House and the Soviet influence campaign for post-war Europe;

- What happens when the full weight of the government is turned against a man of integrity who is "guilty" of telling the truth.

◆

Chapter 2

February 10, 1918
USS Victor
On patrol off Cape May, New Jersey

Under a steel-gray sky, the crew of the *USS Victor,* a 72-foot, 50-ton, wooden-hulled, motor patrol boat was on watch for German submarines at the entrance to Delaware Bay.

The *Victor* patrolled between Cape May, New Jersey and Lewes, Delaware, occasionally venturing upriver as far as Reedy Island. The winter of 1917-18 was the most severe in more than a decade, and Delaware River icepacks were at unprecedented levels, extended for miles seaward.[6]

The deck log for the *Victor* records that at 13:00 hours that Sunday afternoon, the patrol boat stopped and inspected a three-masted schooner sailing out from Puerto Rico and bound for New York City with a cargo of sugar.[7]

At 15:30, without warning, the *Victor's* motor crank case exploded in the engine room, igniting a raging fire. The fire spread quickly, threatening the boat and crew, as the flames extended their reach towards the *Victor's* 1100 gallons of gasoline in its main and reserve tanks. Smoke plumed from the engine room.

The *Victor's* commanding officer, Ensign George H. Earle III and Machinist Mate First Class James J. Logan rushed to the engine room to fight the flames with fire extinguishers. Ensign Earle's fast, clear commands to the *Victor's* complement of ten crew members resulted in the formation of a bucket line from the stern to the engine room. Meanwhile, the remaining hands on deck hoisted an upside-down national ensign and distress signal flags, fired the boat's one 3-inch gun, and sounded the *Victor's* klaxon horn.[8]

Suffering burns, yet still returning to the engine room fire, Earle had ordered the *Victor's* small boat manned, lowered, and sent out for assistance at 15:40. Other crew began to construct a makeshift raft out of doors, tops of berths, hatchways, and tables. Life preservers were on deck. Perhaps more importantly, the crew moved all ammunition (600 rounds for the heavy gun and 6000 rounds for the machine guns)[9] astern to prevent its catching fire and exploding.

Battling a raging fire and overwhelming smoke, Ensign Earle and Machinist Mate Logan returned again and again to the engine compartment in an effort to quench the flames. With the engine inoperable and steerage way lost, the *Victor's* helm did not answer. She was dead in the water and adrift in the currents at the mouth of the bay. At 15:50, "...the fire gained headway, and chances for putting it out looked bad."[10]

Without a wireless radio set, the crew of the *Victor* was at the mercy of the engine room fire, and the near-freezing waters at the mouth of the Delaware River. The air temperature hovered at 34 degrees with moderate southwest winds that February afternoon.

Finally, Earle, Logan and the firefighting crew brought the engine room fire under control by 16:00. The *Victor's* deck log reflects that the fire was completely extinguished by 16:10.[11] Men were posted at stations to watch in case a fresh fire started. The *Victor's* anchor was lowered in order avoid drifting into shallow waters.

Shortly after 17:00, Ensign Earle ordered the "SOS" signal transmitted by "blinker" — a signal lamp producing a pulse of light for Morse Code communications. He also ordered red signal rockets fired over the *Victor*.

At 18:00, the searchlight of the *USS Emerald* (S. P. 177) swept across the *Victor*. By 18:35, the *Emerald* arrived on the scene and began towing the *Victor*. Due to heavy swells running and navigation challenges, the *Emerald* and *Victor* arrived at Cape May at 00:45, November 11. 1918.[12]

For their extraordinary heroism and success at saving the *USS Victor* without loss of life, Ensign George H. Earle III, US Naval Reserve Force and Machinist Mate First Class James J. Logan were both awarded the Navy Cross.[13] At the time of the presentation of the Navy's second highest award for valor (behind only the Medal of Honor), Earle had been promoted to Lieutenant (Junior Grade).

The events of February 1918 were neither the first nor last instances when George Earle exhibited courage, quick thinking and a determined, energetic spirit. Earle had already served on the Mexican border with General John J. "Black Jack" Pershing's Punitive Expedition in 1916 when he enlisted in the Second Pennsylvania Infantry. Within a year, Earle earned a commission as a Pennsylvania National Guard Second Lieutenant.[14]

For the next thirty years, George Earle served Pennsylvania and the United States with distinction and bravery whether in the Pennsylvania governor's mansion, in American embassies overseas, afloat as a Navy gunnery officer, or in Istanbul, Turkey as President Roosevelt's personal emissary in a wartime nest of international intrigue.

Lieutenant (j.g.) George H. Earle III
Courtesy of Melanie Earle Lynagh

***USS Victor* (SP 1995)**
U.S. Naval Historical Center Photograph.
National Archives' Record Group 19-LC

Chapter 3

Philadelphia, Pennsylvania

At the close of World War I, George Earle returned to civilian life. The Earle family traced its lineage back to the *Mayflower's* 1620 landing at Plymouth Rock. When George was born on December 5, 1890 to George H. Earle, Jr., and Catherine Hansell French Earle, he benefitted from the work of several generations of family members who had created enormous wealth and established themselves as persons of prominence and power in the community.[15]

Earle took none of the advantages in life that he enjoyed for granted. Rather, he viewed his position as a charge of responsibility for those less fortunate and to personally serve the nation. Seen by some as a Philadelphia Main Line playboy who enjoyed wine, women and song — he nonetheless was no fool or dilettante. As we will see, George Earle had shrewd political sense, an Everyman quality that endeared him to politicians, bankers, housewives, as well as the steel and coal workers of Pennsylvania. Earle possessed an excellent sense of humor and loved dogs. His energy and optimism were contagious. George Earle was also a man of conviction, who was not afraid to speak his mind and stick to what he believed in, no matter the fashion or consequence. Having volunteered for service on the Mexican border and hunted German submarines off the mid-Atlantic coast, no one could reasonably doubt Earle's personal courage and commitment to public service.

Nonetheless, Earle had his enemies and critics. His energy and impulsiveness did not sit well with the career State Department striped pants set at Foggy Bottom. He upset the machine politics of Pennsylvania, until he started writing sizable checks. His wealth became a point of contention for Republican opponents who called him a Democrat "Sugar Daddy."[16]

Earle never felt constrained. He did whatever he damned well pleased. He drank too much, liked women too much, and said exactly what he thought too much. While others deliberated, he was three steps ahead. He was impatient. It was tough for him to wait on others to catch up to his speed. That conduct drew criticism, jealousy, and attacks. Earle was unfazed and would fight back. Despite his eccentricities, it was very hard not to like George Earle.

Family connections, wealth and power benefitted Earle. The *USS Victor* that he bravely saved on that February afternoon in 1918 was a motor-yacht built in 1917, named after Earle's brother-in-law and owned by Earle's father. The senior Earle leased the *Victor* to the US government for Naval Reserve Force patrol. Likewise, as Earle entered the business world at the end of the war, his wealthy family provided an advantage in Earle's founding of the Flamingo Sugar Mills in Philadelphia. His father seems to have facilitated his role as a director and vice president of the Pennsylvania Sugar Company; a director of the Tradesmen's National Bank and Trust Company; and, a director of the Horn and Hardart Company of New York — the food services company that introduced "automats" to Philadelphia and New York City.[17] These businesses provided a steady revenue stream that allowed Earle to become an extraordinary polo player, sportsman and aviator.

Earle picked-up his civilian life where he left off in 1916 — privileged circumstances where he could indulge his passions and interests. He was, "a young socialite who loved polo ponies, and show dogs, dinner parties and fine wines."[18] Earle had attended

Harvard from 1909 to 1911, but dropped-out to travel for two years in Germany and Austria, then try his hand at business in Chicago. On January 20, 1916, Earle married Huberta F. Potter, a Kentucky belle, with whom he would have four sons: George IV, Hubert, Lawrence and Ralph. Earle's pet nickname for his wife was "Hubie," and despite (or perhaps because of) his reputation as a philanderer, he proclaimed (in 1937) to a gaggle of newsmen, "Boys, I love my wife like nobody's business!"[19]

For roughly a decade, Earle and his family lived in a large, beautiful home on Grays Lane, Haverford, in Lower Merion Township, on the Main Line, west of Philadelphia. The young Earle family had time to pursue their interests at home and abroad. In May 1921, the Earles traveled to Darmstadt, Germany and attended a dog show featuring Doberman Pinschers. An excerpt from the dog-fancier magazine *Dogdom* provides an anecdote that illuminates George Earle's approach to life and, in one sense, foreshadows his future relations with Germans:

> In the possession of two of the most famous Doberman Pinschers, the original German police dogs, in the world, Philadelphia takes precedence over the rest of America, the dog fanciers everywhere have focused their attention and admiration on the two animals in question, which are owned by George H. Earle, 3d, of Haverford.
>
> The most noted of the two dogs is Champion Lord von der Horstburg, to be seen on this month's cover. The other is Champion Centa vom Rinkenbuhl.
>
> A very interesting story lies back of how Mr. and Mrs. Earle, 3d, acquired these two champions when they were in Germany last May. Lord had just taken special for best of both sexes in the Doberman Pinscher show at Darmstadt. No sooner did the owner of Lord realize that an American was inquiring the price of the champion than the figures began to mount. The original price asked for Lord was so high as to mark a record even in these days of high prices that are being paid for bluebloods of

different canine breeds. But Mr. Earle, who is a great admirer of this breed, immediately agreed to pay it. No sooner had it become noised about among the German fanciers present that "the hope of Germany for breeding purposes" had been sold than a riot started in the literal sense of the word. German fanciers flocked about the owner, shook their fists in his face and threatened to attack him if he permitted Lord to be sold to an American.

Immediately Lord's German owner refused to complete the transaction or to accept the price asked. But Mr. Earle, who was determined to bring Lord back to America, made an additional offer of 5000 marks more than the original price agreed upon, and, moreover, took his wallet from his pocket and began to count out the money in good American dollars. Again the owner capitulated and agreed to sell Lord, with a repetition of the scene before enacted immediately following.

The German fanciers and dog show promoters told the owner that never so long as he lived would he again be permitted to show any dog at any German show. He therefore, was again intimidated and returned the money to Mr. Earle, who, with Mrs. Earle, left the confusion and resumed their tour of the interior of Germany.

But Mr. Earle' was determined that America should have that dog, and appointed a special representative to return to the owner of the dog after the show was over with instructions to procure Lord and his mate, Centa, no matter what would be the cost.

Three weeks later negotiations were completed, when double the original price asked for Lord was paid; and a record-breaking price also was paid for Centa. Centa was virtually unknown until she was shown at the great International dog show at Munich. When she was less than thirteen months old she entered the field of 126 entries of Doberman Pinschers and was the sensation of the year, winning the show and becoming red champion for the year 1921—there is only one red champion each year in Germany.[20]

Earle's business holdings prospered through the "Roaring 20s." As vice president of the Pennsylvania Sugar Company, he ran sales up to $80,000,000* per year.[21] *The Philadelphia Inquirer* reported Earle, as captain of the Bryn Mawr Polo Club, traveled to Miami, Florida in January 1925 to join international polo players in the Flamingo Tourneys. *The Inquirer* explained how, "Earle, though one of the youngest players in the country, is one of the most prominent and is rated on par with the Belmonts and others who are considered future international prospects. The local star had his best season last year."[22]

Additional society columns in Philadelphia newspapers and smaller Main Line community papers feature articles and blurbs about the Earle family's departures and returns from various trips, both domestic and abroad. Reports of tea parties, receptions, canasta clubs, galas and dog shows are populated with mentions of the Earles. Sports coverage is replete with George Earle's increasing dominance on the polo grounds and his growing reputation as a world-class player.

The Earle business interests were little affected by the stock market crash and prolonged economic depression leading up to the presidential election of 1932. The 1930 Census documents four live-in servants attending to the Earle household on Grays Lane in Haverford.

The Earle family had long been staunch Republicans, with generations of Earles going back to the 1840s supporting the cornerstone policy on the abolition of slavery. The Earles were not alone. The Commonwealth of Pennsylvania had not had a Democrat governor in 40 years. George H. Earle III would break the mold.

In 1932, Earle switched parties to become a Democrat on the advice of life-long friend William C. Bullitt. Bullitt is a fascinating character in his own right. Another wealthy Philadelphian from the Main Line, Bullitt joined President Woodrow Wilson at Versailles

16

less than six months after graduating from Yale. He was an avowed leftist "progressive" and fan of the Bolsheviks. Under his close friend FDR, Bullitt served as the first US ambassador to the USSR (1933 to 1936), but once exposed to the brutalities of totalitarian communism, he quickly soured on the ideology. Bullitt went on to be the US ambassador to France, but when the Germans marched into Paris in 1940, he refused to leave the city — angering FDR and incurring his presidential wrath. Like Earle, Bullitt would spend the following years as a staunch Cold War anti-communist.

Earle and Bullitt had known each other from their boyhood days at the De Lancey School, a college preparatory in Philadelphia. Each man's competitiveness shines through in the story of a playground fight where Earle beat up Bullitt — only to have Bullitt return the favor following boxing lessons from professional prize fighter Freddie Walsh. Earle and Bullitt would become lifelong friends and political allies.[23]

Earle was drawn to politics during the economic turmoil of the early 1930s, stating, "I kept watching Herbert Hoover's feeble effort to deal with the depression — the puny attempt to let prosperity dribble down from the top … The more I watched, the madder I got."[24]

Earle found easy acceptance into Democrat circles through his affable charm, substantial campaign funding, and like-mindedness with FDR's "New Deal" goals. In a December 2016 interview, 93-year-old Lawrence W. Earle — George's son — said that his father gave FDR "at least $50,000[†] and probably a hell of a lot more than that." We do know that George Earle gave the Pennsylvania State and Philadelphia Democratic committees at least $140,000[‡].[25]

Besides the cash infusion to the party, Earle contributed his energy and natural leadership abilities. He mobilized people, especially Main Line socialites who were naturally leery of FDR's brand of socialism. Earle could stir-up a crowd, and the party relied upon him and his excellent public speaking skills. With the election results of 1932, George Earle's prominent support of FDR resulted in his appointment as the "Envoy Extraordinary and Minister Plenipotentiary to the Republic of Austria" on July 24, 1933.[26]

Centa Vom Rinkenbuhl, 1921
Red Doberman Pinscher
Champion Of Germany
Imported by George H. Earle III
Dogdom Magazine[ii]

George H. Earle III (1933)
Courtesy of
Melanie Earle Lynagh

[ii] ✳ $1,116,450,000 in 2017 dollars; † $730,000 in 2017 dollars; ‡ $2,050,000 in 2017 dollars.

Chapter 4

Vienna, Austria

The American minister's residence on *Argentinierstraße* was the *palais* of an Austrian prince. It was two short blocks from Belvedere, the Baroque, 18th-century, Austro-Hungarian imperial palace. The Earle family decamped from Philadelphia to Vienna, arriving in the autumn of 1933. What Lawrence Earle, then 9-years old, loved most about their new Viennese home was the elevator, the nearby *"schwimmbad "* indoor swimming pool with a wave machine, and when his older brother, George IV, would flood the bricked courtyard in winter and create their own ice-skating rink.[27] The four Earle boys were learning to enjoy life as their father did.

After presenting his credentials to the Austrian government on September 27, 1933, and fulfilling the diplomatic niceties required by protocol, Earle got to work. By late October 1933, Earle set off on a 14-day "trip of observation through 9 Austrian provincial capitals calling on governors and officials."[28] He was accompanied by Alfred W. Kliefoth, First Secretary of the Legation and Lieutenant Colonel Martin C. Shallenberger, the Military Attaché.

Earle was proud of his tour of the Austrian provinces. He wrote of the warm receptions his small party received and bragged mildly in a dispatch that his trip had been, "the first time any foreign diplomat had called" [on provincial officials].[29]

The new American minister walked into a hornet's nest of political brinksmanship that could easily have erupted into war. Nazi

Germany was consistently making aggressive moves against Austria. The National Socialist Party of Austria was clearly taking directions from Berlin and agitating — sometimes violently — for an *Anschluß* (political union with Germany through annexation, that would eventually be realized in March 1938). The Nazi government kept up a steady radio propaganda campaign aimed at destabilizing the legitimate Austrian government. Here is an excerpt of a Nazi broadcast from September 8, 1933:

> Our German brothers in Austria stand in the midst of their battle for liberation. The separatist Dollfuss Government defends itself desperately by means of terror, lies, violation of the constitution, and betrayal of the people. The Nazi Party of Austria has been forbidden all political activity! All propaganda for Germany is brutally suppressed! There are no longer any national newspapers. On the other hand the Jewish papers of all system parties [sic] carry on a tremendous campaign of lies against Adolf Hitler and Nazi Germany.
>
> … To work, fellow citizens! It is a question of the maintenance of Germanism in Austria! Strengthen our brothers in their defensive battle! Faithful unto victory![30]

Austria was ruled by the diminutive Chancellor Englebert Dollfuß, who teetered precariously between the Austrian Nazis and the Social Democrats — all while trying to implement economic confidence building measures and repay national debts. Dollfuß may not have been the ideal national leader, as he exercised semi-dictatorial control of the government, but he was certainly considered the last refuge of democratic, classic liberalism for Austria.

Earle's early reports to Washington, DC stressed the desperate need for economic development in Austria. He reported that it was the greatest danger to the government and the country's continued democratic independence. Earle was a true friend to

Austria and personally encouraged the creation of a trade delegation to drum up business and tourism from the United States. Years later, as governor of Pennsylvania, Earle received letters of thanks and praise for his service in Vienna. The volume and tone of correspondence maintained in the Pennsylvania State Archives in Harrisburg are proof that Earle made a strong, lasting, and favorable impression on the Austrian people.

As minister, Earle played an important foreign policy role in sounding the alarm over the dangers of Nazism, warning the Austrian government that it would lose American sympathy if Austrians encouraged the spread of anti-Semitism. In a cable to Jay Pierrepont Moffat, the Chief of the Division of Western European Affairs on November 21, 1933, Earle made his position clear:

> Since we have several hundred American Jews here, and since Austrians are like Freshmen at college who prefer popularity to anything else, I thought an ounce of prevention might save a hell of a lot of trouble later, so in my statement to the press after my trip through Austria I said that since 90% of all Americans were themselves, or were descended from, people who came to America to escape racial or religious persecution, the sympathy of the American people would not be with any country that indulged in such persecution. In absolute confidence the Dollfuss Government told me my statement had strengthened their hands in dealing with this issue.[31]

Earle's pronouncement rejecting anti-Semitism did not go unnoticed. The United Press wire service reported Earle's statement as: "To numerous important personages in the course of a tour in Austria, I said the surest way to alienate the United States' present sympathy for Austria would be to start an anti-Semitic movement."[32]

As one might expect, the Nazi press and their affiliates either ignored Earle's statement or vilified him. The Nazi attacks were the first of several more to come during George Earle's service in Vienna; Sofia, Bulgaria; and, Istanbul, Turkey.

As Earle closed out his November cable to Moffat, he demonstrated how his independence and initiative would be an unconventional irritant to the professional diplomats at the State Department. Imagine the reaction of bureaucrats and desk officers reading a cable from Earle when it dawns on them that Earle personally possessed a level of political and economic capital beyond their control (and perhaps, beyond their understanding). He was independent. Earle makes his economic case to Moffat in terms that do not allow for a negative response:

> Now, Pierrepont, I believe the following absolutely: first, that the peace of Europe depends on Austria's independence. Second, that Austria's independence depends entirely on an improvement in economic conditions here. Dollfuss also firmly believes this.

> Before I left America I talked to ten of the biggest bankers, publicists, and merchants. They were all eager to help Austria by buying her goods, wines, etc. Austria, in turn, learning of my desire to improve trade conditions, showed her willingness to reciprocate by taking off all restrictions on our apples. Austria has fine wines, liqueurs, leather goods, etc., at a much lower figure than any other country that I know of.

> Dollfuss, realizing his only hope of remaining in power lies in improving Austria's trade, is very anxious for me to go back to America and start things rolling, with or without, as you think best, an Austrian business committee of two or three men in January or February.

> Words of sympathy are all right, but only improvement in trade is going to save Austria.

> For these reasons I would like very much for you to order me back for a conference, leaving it to me whether it would be in January or February . . . .

In any case, order me back because I have had enough business experience to know I can get results in America for Austria.[33]

What an astounding cable! The career bureaucrats in the State Department were certain to be either appalled grievously or stunned catatonically. Earle's initiative and independence were not welcome at Foggy Bottom.

Let us pause here and consider Earle's circumstances set against the context of the foreign policy position of the United States vis-a-vis Central Europe in late 1933 and early 1934. The fundamental grievances and incendiaries of what would become World War II were swirling around Earle. The United States had returned to being a slumbering giant – largely isolationist from a bitter World War I experience and in the throes of the Great Depression. FDR was struggling through his first term, though hagiographies largely ignore his unpopularity at this point. Earle is a practical and successful businessman who believes he can push back hard against Nazis and Communists alike by giving the Austrians a fighting chance through economic development. The State Department is not quite sure exactly what "economic development" means. This instance in time and the contemporaneous documentary evidence of State Department cables are another chapter of "Lost History" to most Americans – who are educated and led to believe that the WWII "happened" without the knowledge of FDR and official Washington DC. Here are the lessons Earle could have taught FDR and the State Department, if they were willing to listen: Dollfuß did not have to die. *Anschluß* was no surprise.

George Earle began a 60-day leave period in the United States beginning January 16, 1934. Earle's leave would be cut in half because of revolutionary crisis in Austria. Nonetheless, the Austrian government followed Earle's lead and dispatched an Austrian Trade Commission to America on February 15, 1934.

Three of the members included the president of the Boehler Foundry Company, the president of the largest textile enterprise, and Count Seefried, a great-grandson of Emperor Francis Joseph. Earle demonstrated how to get results in America for Austria — and *vice versa*.[34]

Earle's departure for the United States was not simply to bolster Austrian trade opportunities and help stabilize the economy of the besieged country. He had his own motives as well. The leadership of the Democratic Party of Pennsylvania was meeting and formulating their slate of candidates for the May primary and November 1934 general elections. The political and ideological balance struck by party leaders for the governor – lieutenant governor ticket was remarkable. Gubernatorial nominee George Earle, as the wealthy scion of a prominent Philadelphia family, matched with Thomas Kennedy, the secretary-treasurer of the United Mine Workers of America. Interestingly, Kennedy would hold his union post concurrent with his service as lieutenant governor.[35] The match was perfect political marketing and aimed at appealing to the general electorate through the strengths of each candidate. The party was probably further motivated by Earle's checkbook, but no specific dollar figures can be attributed to this brief visit by Earle.

Within a week of Earle's departure from Vienna for the United States, all hell broke loose in Austria. Austria began openly discussing a protest with the League of Nations about Germany's conduct towards her and Berlin's meddling in domestic Austrian political affairs. There was a divergence of opinions among western European powers on the forum and process by which to call attention to German meddling.

As though to rub salt in the Austrian wounds, on January 28th German officials sponsored a charity benefit concert in Berlin held under the auspices of the *Kampfring der Deutsch-Oesterreichischer im Reich* ("Battle ring of the German-Austrians in the Reich"), with the proceeds used for support of the Austrian National Socialists.[36]

Over February 12th and 13th, US Chargé Alfred Kliefoth cabled disturbing reports on the Austrian domestic political scene from Vienna back to Washington:

> *The* action of *the* police *in Linz in* searching Socialist *headquarters this morning* resulted *in* bloodshed and *martial law* where*upon Vienna's* electric workmen called strike in sympathy cutting *off* electric *light* and streetcar *transportation* and *industries* dependent *upon* electric *power. Streets are* patrolled by police armed with carbines.

And,

> The Socialist strike in Vienna developed into general Socialist revolt all over Austria against the Government but which found little public sympathy ... The suppressed revolt of the Socialist[s] means that Dollfuss will no longer enjoy their tolerance in his fight against the Nazis. No reports of Americans injured or molested.[37]

As this crisis unfolded, Secretary of State Cordell Hull became increasingly concerned over the dearth of reporting from Vienna. He clearly expected more information from Kliefoth on a situation that many believed could be a 1934 version of Sarajevo. On February 15, 1934, Hull cabled Kliefoth: "Please report more frequently during this crisis including pertinent information on the welfare of Americans in Austria – Hull."[38] That same day, George Earle was ordered off leave and immediately back to Austria to protect American interests.

The Austrian Socialists' advanced military preparations caught the government off-guard. The Socialist resistance put up an organized resistance from fortified dwellings resulting in unexpectedly high casualties on both sides. Let us be clear: this is urban combat. At one point, Socialist machine-gunners were facing government artillery direct-fire in an effort to breach their strongpoints. That means firing cannons into apartment blocks. Dollfuß had to rely on the *Heimwehr* (Home Army) fascist stormtroopers armed and trained over a period of ten years by Prince von Starhemberg, the 34-year old head of one of the richest and most powerful families in Austria. The *Heimwehr* doubled Dollfuß's overall strength to approximately 44,000 men, but with political strings attached.

Earle's first cable back to Washington, DC from Vienna was a proposed press statement that was nothing short of brilliant, given his hurried return from Washington and the violence in the Vienna. Earle made the effort to clear his statements, which enjoyed a full endorsement from the Austrian foreign ministry, with the Washington bureaucrats. Once again, we can see how Earle's instincts and initiative terrified the State Department establishment, while being clear, direct and historically prescient:

863.00/882: Telegram

The Minister in Austria (Earle) to the Secretary of State
VIENNA, February 28, 1934-noon.

[Received February 28-9:45 a. m.]

37. The press here are insisting on an interview. The reasons for giving it are (1) to help heal the wounds of the uprising of February 12, (2) to encourage Dollfuss in granting even more clemency to 1,800 Socialist prisoners and, (3) to reiterate President Roosevelt's words regarding the results of militarism in Europe. Unless I am informed you have objections I will issue the following statement March 1st, 1 p.m.

I have seen the places where the really serious fighting took place and talked to many eye witnesses. I have two outstanding impressions.

First. The magnificent courage displayed by every Austrian engaged in the actual conflict.

Secondly. The fine clemency shown by the victorious Government forces who have not forgotten to be merciful to their defeated but brave brother Austrians whom, in defense of the Fatherland, they know would march shoulder to shoulder with them.

I have just come from America. It is almost impossible to believe that such a change for the better could take place in the 5 months I have been away. Everyone there is cheerful and prosperity is coming back in leaps and bounds under the leadership of our great President. Provided all the nations of Europe will take heed of what our President has pointed out and dispel the constant paralyzing menace of war by respecting and acknowledging the boundaries and the duties of other nations there will be an economic revival in Europe amazing in its extent. If Europe is not able to accompany-America back on the road to happiness and prosperity let the burden and blame for this rest squarely upon that nation or nations who constantly rattles the sword in the scabbard and by direct or implied threat keeps all Europe in uncertainty and suspense of an offensive war that will engulf the Continent. ["]

EARLE[39]

The State Department response was swift. Inside Washington, this was precisely the sort of overseas cable that makes the career bureaucracy uneasy, if not hostile. The sender, in this case Minister Earle, cited outside forces (the press) and formulated a response (actually, his own ideas on policies) and then set the timer on a "ticking time bomb" (an instruction cable deadline of March 1st at 1p.m.). Failure to respond by the State Department was tacit permission for Minister Earle to do as he saw fit. Under ordinary conditions, the State Department would have spent days – perhaps weeks – crafting each word of a very deliberate press statement. George Earle was giving the Secretary of State Cordell Hull a little more than 24-hours to get back to him. Earle was interested in being effective, timely and supportive of Dollfuß. Secretary Hull had no interest in George Earle encouraging anyone to do anything, not even efforts at clemency and reconciliation:

> 863.00/882: Telegram
>
> The Secretary of State to the Minister in Austria (Earle)
> WASHINGTON February 28, 1934-4 p.m.
>
> 11. Your 37, February 28, noon, and your 38. I have personally gone over your proposed statement and discussed it with Phillips and with other collaborators here. We are unanimously of the opinion that it would be misunderstood (a) in Europe, where it might be read as implying American aid against an aggressor, and (b) in this country where it would be considered an intervention in European political affairs. For these reasons I feel that it would be better to confine any interview you may give to the press to an analysis of economic conditions in the United States.
>
> Hull[40]

Hull could not have been any more wrong – but it was the Washington Establishment vs. the millionaire playboy political benefactor – so Earle would have to express himself in other ways.

Fresh on the scene back in Austria, Earle wasted no time touring the areas most affected by the uprising and speaking to Austrian officials at all levels. That is a demonstration of Earle's personal, physical courage in carrying out his duties. It is no different from Earle's running into the burning engine room of the *USS Victor*. Earle could have sat in the embassy and reviewed reports. Instead, he went out into the areas of combat, placing himself physically between Nazis and Communists who were only just machine-gunning each other, lobbing grenades and fighting house-to-house. He engaged the people on the ground; did his own interviews; and, brought his own brand of diplomatic reporting back to Washington, DC.

In his cable back to Washington, Earle graciously cites the work of First Secretary Kliefoth and his military attaché, Colonel Shallanberger. He compliments the quality of their insights and reporting. Again, Earle composes a cable with remarkable political, military, economic and social insights concerning the situation facing the Austrian government and its people:

863.00/8811: Telegram

The Minister in Austria (Earle) to the Secretary of State
VIENNA, March 2, 1934-noon.

[Received 12:20 p. m.]

39. I have just returned from tour of the districts of Vienna involved in the uprising and questioned many eyewitnesses. While it is impossible for me to interview the leaders of the uprising I have seen and heard enough to obtain a fairly clear picture of the situation …

The clemency shown by the Chancellor is amazing. The relief and aid given to the insurgents' families by Dollfuss is almost unparalleled in Europe. He bitterly regrets the necessity of the use of artillery against the semi-fortified machine nests in workers houses.

However, had the Government given the insurrectionists longer time to organize the Nazis would have started a simultaneous attack and Austria would now be under Hitler's control in actuality if not in name …

I believe Dollfuss' position is stronger than ever and that conditions are less threatening and more stable than at any time since my arrival last September. This opinion is directly contradicted by foreign press representatives who unanimously agree that Dollfuss is greatly directly weakened by the loss of Socialist support, lukewarm though it was …

An interesting side light is that a few nights ago the Soviet radio in Leningrad vilified the Austrian Socialists for their failure to support the uprising …

Dollfuss' real weakness was the attacks against him in the foreign press which have now let up. If he had given way to these attacks the blame for establishing Hitlerism in Austria would have rested on the foreign correspondents who grossly misrepresented the situation.

EARLE[41]

Earle is not alone in his criticism of the foreign correspondents covering the revolt in Austria. A few days earlier, while Kliefoth was still acting as the Chargé during Earle's leave in the US, the Austrian Foreign Ministry had complained bitterly about how the American press was covering this violent crisis.[42] These criticisms reflect back on Hull's timid error in preventing Earle from issuing a strong press statement upon his return to Vienna.

A few days later in March of 1934, George Earle tendered his resignation as Minister to Austria to FDR in order to return to the United States and run for Governor of Pennsylvania. Earle was succeeded in Vienna by George Strausser Messersmith, who had been serving in Berlin as the counsel general under Ambassador Dodd.

Earle's decision to resign was driven, in part, by timing. The Democratic primary was May 15th and although Earle enjoyed party backing on the slate of candidates, there were some Democrats who were critical of him and willing to go through a primary challenge. Given trans-Atlantic travel times and the move of his entire household, Earle needed to get home and get on the campaign trail.

Earle's warm relationship with Dollfuß is reflected in his March 23, 1934 letter informing the chancellor of the relinquishment of his post as minister:

> I leave Austria with feelings of great regret, just as though I were leaving a friend. When I arrived in Austria last year I already had some knowledge of the beauty of the country and the charm of the people, but I failed to realize the extent of the real greatness of the Austrian people. I

shall consider it my bounden duty to acquaint the people of the United States with this fact and to assist them in finding opportunity to learn more about Austria.

I will consider the opportunity of having known you personally, Mr. Chancellor, as one of the greatest privileges of my life, and am looking forward to your continued success.[43]

Four months later, on July 25th, Dollfuß would be shot dead by ten Austrian Nazis in the Chancellery building.

Engelbert Dollfuß
Time **magazine, September 25 1933**

Envoy Ordered Back

George Earle

Here is George Earle, American minister to Austria, who has been ordered by President Roosevelt to cut short his stay in the United States and return immediately to Austria to protect American interests in the current disorders between government forces and Socialists.

44

Chapter 5

Harrisburg, Pennsylvania

Governor-elect and Mrs. George H. Earle came to the brownstone executive mansion on Front Street in Harrisburg with four bustling boys and several dogs, including Mrs. Earle's favorite champion poodle, Gentleman Harpindale Swank ("Swanky"). Earle's victory had been by a relatively slim 66,000 votes – but that is not terribly surprising given he was the first Democrat elected governor of Pennsylvania since 1895. Republicans enjoyed a registration lead of 1.22 million voters, so from the very start it was an uphill, hard-fought campaign. Roosevelt did not win Pennsylvania in the 1932 election, but Earle pulled off a victory in 1934.

With FDR at his side on a snowy January 15, 1935, 44-year old George H. Earle III took the oath of office as Governor of the Commonwealth of Pennsylvania. He acknowledged in his inaugural address that, "these are desperately trying times, bitter times." Earle also made a statement that demonstrated a keen self-awareness of his personal strengths and weaknesses. It is a remarkably important personal declaration that serves as a rhetorical lens through which to observe and evaluate George Earle, the man. Earle stated: "I will make mistakes, I know, but they will be mistakes of the head and not of the heart."[45]

Earle began his campaign while on leave from his duties as Minister to Austria. His time off from the revolutionary turmoil in Vienna was spent promoting an Austrian trade junket to the US, but it also neatly coincided with the meeting of Pennsylvania Democratic party chieftains, such as long-time state party leader Joe Guffey, publisher David Stern, contractors Matthew McCoskey, John B. Kelly and Democratic State Chairman David Lawrence. Stern was the publisher of *The Philadelphia Record* and the *New York Post*. Contractor McCloskey was the inventor of the now-standard American political fundraiser event: the $100-a-plate dinner, and Kelly was a former bricklayer who ended up ousting Philadelphia Democratic Party boss John O'Donnell. Earle first came the attention of Guffey in 1932 based on his substantial contributions to FDR. [46] The party slate drawn up in January featured Earle for Governor, Thomas Kennedy, secretary-treasurer of the United Mine Workers for lieutenant governor, and Joe Guffey for US Senate.

Earle was to be the New Deal face of the Democratic Party of Pennsylvania. His ability to finance his own campaign operations added to his appeal. Having supported FDR substantially in the last election cycle, Earle was also closely identified with the New Deal administration – and that connection was a major theme in the gubernatorial election. Campaign posters and advertisements equated voting for Earle as a vote for FDR, and *vice versa*.

Earle had enemies within the Pennsylvania Democratic Party that resented him personally and professionally. Long-time party members who had paid their dues, literally and figuratively – and those who were not comfortable with the millionaire playboy. After all, he was a polo player! He seemed too white-collar, too Republican, too rich. These concerns and suspicions fell by the wayside with Earle's clear and convincing dedication to the New Deal philosophy. Earle also put his money where his mouth was – and that was a special evidence that proved difficult to dismiss or doubt.

Republican opponents of Earle banged the same rhetorical drums. Republican Senator David A. Reed (attorney for the Mellon family of Pittsburgh and their substantial corporate interests) sought to paint Earle as financially irresponsible and lacking good judgment. On October 2, 1934 in a speech in Lancaster, PA, Reed impugned Earle by claiming that his father had established a "spendthrift trust" for his son. A spendthrift trust is a legal and financial device created for the benefit of a person (often unable to control his spending) that gives an independent trustee full authority to make decisions as to how the trust funds may be spent for the beneficiary. Two nights later, Democratic State Chairman David Lawrence took to the radio airwaves across Pennsylvania in defense of George Earle and called Reed a "liar." Lawrence went further, challenging anyone to examine the will of George Earle, Jr. and see the truth for themselves, as it was a public document. Lawrence cast Reed's reckless language as the act of someone that was panic stricken and certain of an overwhelming defeat.[47] Such was the political environment and the rhetorical attacks waged against Earle from all sides in his campaign for governor.

Home in Haverford only a short while, Earle learned of the murder of Austrian Chancellor Engelbert Dollfuß in late July 1934. Again, Earle made a clear stand against Hitler and Nazi efforts to dominate his recent diplomatic posting, calling his friend's death,

> Cold-blooded murder, undoubtedly inspired by Hitler's terrorizing action ... The killing of Dollfuss will defeat the very purpose its leaders had hoped to achieve. It will create a feeling against the Nazis among those lukewarm, those on the fence, and those who might have adopted the movement.[48]

Pennsylvania politics did not call for much foreign policy expertise, but as Earle's gubernatorial campaign began in earnest, turbulence in Europe – and in Vienna – offered Earle an opportunity to demonstrate his expertise and insights on foreign policy. His enemies attacked Earle, claiming he had abandoned his post at precisely the moment he was most needed in order to pursue selfish personal political aspirations.

There is documentary evidence of the disdain the professional political *brahmans* of the State Department felt towards Earle. In a November 1, 1934 memorandum from Jay Pierrepont Moffat, the Chief of the Division of Western European Affairs to Minister George S. Messersmith (Earle's replacement in Vienna) Moffat wrote:

> Your predecessor, George Earle, was down here for a day or two and asked for the latest news of Austria. He is waging a hot political fight, though most of my Pennsylvania friends do not feel that he will succeed in the elections. He has a strong opponent, Schnader, against him.[49]

In context, one may infer a sneering tone of *schadenfreude* towards Earle in Moffat's letter.

Nonetheless, in July 1934, Earle's frank assessment of European affairs was correct: "The most bloody war in the world's history [as a result of Chancellor Dollfuß's assassination] unless national ambitions [are] shelved in all Europe."[50] It would take five more years for the outbreak of war, but George Earle saw it coming clearly.

The situation in Pennsylvania was desperate. The commonwealth's industrial output had plummeted by more than 50% between 1929 and 1932. One-third of the Pennsylvania's wage-earners were without any source on income by 1932.[51] Nearly one-third of all the homes in Philadelphia were auctioned off for tax and mortgage defaults. More than 400 Pennsylvania banks folded or were forced to merge. Pennsylvania, while still a wealthy state, lacked sufficient statutory social support processes for programs like workmen's compensation, unemployment, as well as widows and orphans' compensation.[52]

FDR's New Deal in Washington, DC drew greater and greater support from varying blocks of voters in Pennsylvania who had traditionally been Republican. Lending assistance and government assistance programs in both urban and rural districts of Pennsylvania were materially persuasive to voters. First and second-generation ethnic immigrant communities – the so-called "hyphen groups" – had started to move Democratic as early as 1928. African-Americans abandoned the "Party of Lincoln" for FDR. These broad demographic and political shifts were realized and authenticated by the election of Earle.[53]

Governor Earle's "Little New Deal" for the Commonwealth of Pennsylvania quickly caught on as the tag line and description for the Earle administration's policies and programs. The country already had a two-year orientation to the types of government assistance available under FDR's administration, so the philosophy of a state level program was quickly and easily understood – even if the details had yet to be ironed out. Ironically, the term "Little New Deal" started out as a pejorative smear against Governor Earle by hostile reporters and press. Instead it was the perfect political summary for a new administration.[54]

Governor Earle's political victory on November 6, 1934 also delivered the Pennsylvania House to the Democrats, but the Senate remained in Republican hands. To successfully implement his unemployment relief and other programs, Earle proposed a $203,000,000 tax increase. He sought to raise money through tax increases on gasoline, personal property and utilities, while adding new taxes on the income of corporations, chain retail outlets, cigarettes, and other amusements. [55] The Republicans in the Pennsylvania Senate raised immediate and loud protests against Earle's proposal. The Chamber of Commerce joined the chorus of criticism, claiming that, "the sun and the air would be made targets for taxation."[56]

Earle's inaugural address made clear points that his administration would deliver on:

"I believe in work relief rather than the dole ... We will care for the unemployed, but let us beware of creating unemployables. [and] Child labor must never return."[57] Earle's record of success on delivering the reforms and relief he promised was remarkable. His achievements included: the Pennsylvania Turnpike; stringent child labor laws; the Department of Public Assistance; state responsibility for the mentally ill; teacher tenure; milk price controls; election law reform; a revised divorce code; labor benefits and unemployment compensation; the elimination of strike breakers and the notorious "Coal and Iron Police."[58] Earle also relaxed Pennsylvania's "Blue Laws" to allow people to go to the movies or enjoy fishing on Sundays.

Perhaps most remarkable for the time, Earle signed an "equal rights" bill in 1935 that, "enables any Negro in Pennsylvania to bring suit for damages if he is discriminated against by a hotel, restaurant, shop, or theatre."[59] Earle worked actively with North Carolina-born, African-American state legislator Hobson Reynolds, who introduced the bill.[60] In this regard, George Earle was 30-years ahead of the rest of the country. This was yet another moment wherein Earle demonstrated the courage of his personal convictions. He had no "need" to expend personal and Democratic political capital on such a progressive reform. He did it because it was right.

Getting to all of those accomplishments was not easy. In late April 1935, Governor Earle summoned the leadership of the hostile Republican Senate to a closed-door meeting on a tax compromise. Earle's $203,000,000 tax increase with 22 points for relief and programs was diametrically opposite of the rival Senate plan for a nine-point $111,500,000 program. Earle did not pull any rhetorical political punches in setting the tone for his negotiations with the Republican Senate leadership. Earle called the Senate opposition "a smoke screen and a camouflage to distract public attention while the social and labor program is being done to death." He added, "I am not only prepared but anxious to meet such of the enlightened and liberal Republican members of the Senate whose consciences recognize the evils of the destructive and obstructive tactics pursued by their tory leadership."[61]

The "enlightened and liberal Republicans" split from their caucus and delivered Governor Earle a compromise victory, in which the governor won many of the programs he sought. This established a pattern that would repeat itself. A record 3,514 bills were introduced in the state legislature in Earle's first two years.[62] Although the Republican Senate blocked many bills, a significant number also passed.

A vexing problem for Governor Earle was Pennsylvania's "bootleg coal" operations. By 1935, more than 10,000 jobless miners were eking out a living mining coal on abandoned coal company properties. The bootleggers openly defied the law and property rights, digging in "dog holes" to exploit the remaining coal reserves in closed mineshafts. Earle went out to the counties of western Pennsylvania most affected by the coal company shut-downs and the resultant bootlegging. He visited mines, homes, churches and chambers of commerce. Local residents gave Earle an earful of criticism against the seven coal companies that owned 85% of the anthracite coal in the western hemisphere. A local sheriff admitted to Governor Earle that he had taken little action against the bootleggers because he felt they were morally justified. Governor Earle told the sheriff his actions were, "very humane, but very illegal."[63]

The coal companies pointed to a 50% loss of market and profits that were small or non-existent. Within a couple of days of his trip to anthracite country, Governor Earle set clear objectives for resolving the bootlegging crisis. He acknowledged that the illicit practice must end in order to preserve the basic tenets of law and order, even though he was sympathetic to the human struggle for survival. Importantly, he definitively barred the use of force in clearing bootleggers from mining property, declaring it was "out of the question."[64] Earle promised and then appointed a commission with broad powers to study the bootlegging problem and make recommendations, but in practical terms, he did little to stop it.

Earle was periodically attacked for his hands-off approach to the bootlegging problem. He survived a half-hearted effort to impeach him by Republicans who used the lingering crisis for political leverage. Support for Earle's compromise solutions from both the coal industry and state legislature was elusive. He offered options for the state to buy the unused mining lands and for the creation of a "co-op market." His ideas were rejected. Finally, in desperation, he sought assistance from FDR for a federal takeover.[65] Each initiative dead-ended in intransigence. Bootleg mining continued unabated.

Almost two years into his term, Governor Earle sat with Lawrence Davies of the *New York Times* for an interview. Written as a biographic profile, "A Political Star Rises in Pennsylvania" provides important insight into Earle's motivation and success personally, professionally and as a public servant. Asked to define his political philosophy, Earle was refreshingly frank:

> It is a philosophy of liberalism. It is a philosophy that demands that one must strive constantly to attain, as nearly as possible, fair play and equal opportunity for all. In other words, any man or group that likes fair play doesn't need fear me. Otherwise, they need fear me a great deal.[66]

Earlier in the year, Earle served as host for the 1936 Democratic National Convention in Philadelphia. At the encouragement of Governor Earle, Reverend Marshall Lorenzo Shepard, the first African-American elected as a Democrat to the

Pennsylvania legislature, was also the first African-American to deliver the opening invocation at the Democratic National presidential convention.[67] Once again, Earle's personal conviction to equal justice under the law was highlighted by this important demonstration reinforcing the prior year's equal rights law. The re-nomination of FDR and overwhelming success of the event reflected great credit and importance upon the personal prestige and political horsepower of Governor Earle. Press referred to Earle as FDR's "fair-haired boy," and much was made of the two men's personal friendship, Harvard education, similar family wealth and backgrounds, as well as their important political alliance. No one missed the significance of George H. Earle III providing substantial financial backing to FDR for his 1932 election, and then hosting the incumbent president's national convention in Earle's home city.

In June 1937, Governor Earle stepped into the midst of a steel strike at Bethlehem Steel's Cambria Plant in Johnstown, PA.

Earle's first concern was preventing violence and loss of life, as well as private property. He declared a form of martial law, dispatching the state police and placing them under the command of Colonel A.S. Janeway, a Pennsylvania National Guard officer and Director of the General State Authority. He also asked Cambria Plant executives to close the steel plant, upon learning that 40,000 members of the United Mine Workers were to march on Johnstown. Governor Earle came under direct and bitter attack from all sides because of his actions. He was accused of being heavy-handed and exceeding his police authorities; of disrespecting the private property and business rights of Bethlehem Steel; and, of being a "labor governor" who was a strikebreaker. The *New York Herald Tribune* went so far as to claim:

> The government of Pennsylvania has gone into action in full military support of labor gangsterism on a gigantic scale. Further comment on such a situation is futile. It not only speaks for itself; it shrieks for the attention of the whole nation.

And,

> ...Governor Earle the rich, lily-handed, exploiter of class warfare, who hopes to succeed Mr. Roosevelt in the White House, to move openly and defiantly into the camp of the C.I.O. [Congress of Industrial Organizations] terrorists and to offer them the support of Pennsylvania's state police and militia at need.[68]

Earle addressed the hyperbole of the *Herald Tribune* and other criticisms by saying:

> In this crisis, the choice to be made was lives or dollars. I chose lives, and acted accordingly. After four days of enforced peace, to think it over, I hope the forces of labor and capital in Johnstown will make the same decision.[69]

In fact, Governor Earle's assessment was correct, indicating that his original instincts concerning the dangers posed to the community warranted his extraordinary action and set the tone for a law-and-order solution. Unfortunately, two weeks later, labor operatives dynamited the Cambria mill's water supply.

"Stamp those Goddam Communists out of the Labor movement!" cried Labor-loving Gov. George Earle of Pennsylvania to steel strikers & sympathizers at Johnstown July 4. 70

Speculation swirled in political and newspaper circles about a 1938 senatorial run for Earle, and a 1940 presidential campaign. George Earle seemed FDR's heir apparent. Asked by Lawrence Davies of the *New York Times* to speculate on his future intentions, Earle said:

> Too many good governors have been ruined [by their political ambitions]. To be perfectly frank, my philosophy is to do the best you can, but expect very little, and you won't be disappointed. I have no illusions about popular favor. It comes and goes like an April shower.[71]

Nonetheless, at FDR's inaugural parade, in a downpour when Earle alone among 30 governors, rode like the President in an open car, nodding and beaming at the crowd among whom groups from Pennsylvania shouted, "Our next president!"[72]

In the same Davies interview, we get another glimpse of Earle's independence and personal convictions. One might think that given Earle's clear connection with FDR and the New Deal, he would be a staunch, dyed-in-the-wool "party man." No. Earle made a nuanced but clear distinction about the subject of party politics and individual conscience. He valued political independents over party ideologues. Earle said:

> I feel that a man may change his political parties as often as he wishes, if he doesn't change his principles. I never have been prominent in politics. I had been an independent Republican all my life, but I felt that President Hoover, in pouring in money from the top, and hoping that it would trickle down, was pursuing an entirely wrong principle. The independents, in my opinion, are the people we have to depend upon.[73]

Despite Democratic party legislative successes and the implementation of Governor Earle's Little New Deal reforms, the political tide turned in 1938. Success caught up with the Democrats. Earle was precluded by statute from a second consecutive term. Internecine primary fights consumed political capital. The fatal blow came from Governor Earle's (former Republican) Attorney General Charles Margiotti.

Margiotti was seeking the Democratic primary nomination to succeed Earle as governor. His problem was that he could not gain the endorsement of the sitting governor, the state party chairman or the incumbent Democratic senator. Margiotti began making statements about public corruption issues pertaining to the administration of contracts for highways and roads. Less than a month before the Democratic primary, Governor Earle fired Margiotti as Attorney General. That act provoked the Dauphin County (Harrisburg) District Attorney Carl Shelley to immediately impanel a grand jury and begin an investigation seeking indictments. Governor Earle called Shelley's move, "A shameless political conspiracy engineered by the Republican leadership ... a barrage of poison gas ... rumors, hearsay and gossip."[74]

Governor Earle went on the offensive, convening a special session of the legislature and demanding a legislative investigation to prevent Shelley's politically motivated "harassment." Earle got everything he asked for from the legislature. Shelley's grand jury was disestablished by law; the legislature reserved the right to investigate impeachable offenses; the attorney general was explicitly granted the right to supersede any county district attorney's actions; and, a House committee was formed to investigate the corruption charges and jail uncooperative witnesses. This lightning action by Governor Earle drew immediate comparisons to the "dictatorial" powers of Louisiana Governor Huey "The Kingfish" Long.[75]

Governor Earle was never indicted. When the smoke cleared, Shelley conceded that he had no personal knowledge of Earle administration misdeeds. Three minor officials received fines and one spent 60 days in jail. Democratic Party leader Dave Lawrence claimed vindication for the Earle administration and all of his colleagues, but the damage was done. Earle Democrats were beaten badly in 1938. Governor Earle himself lost his Senate bid by nearly 400,000 votes and only carried four counties.[76]

Thus, ended another phase of the remarkable life of George H. Earle III. While all that Earle had experienced up until 1938 may have been enough for two or even three lives of ordinary people – George Earle was just getting started.

**Inauguration of Pennsylvania Governor George H. Earle III with
President Franklin Delano Roosevelt, Harrisburg, PA, January 15, 1935.
Courtesy of Melanie Earle Lynagh.**

**Governor George Howard Earle III
Courtesy of Melanie Earle Lynagh**

October 1936: President Franklin Delano Roosevelt in Harrisburg, PA for a political rally. Governor George Earle, who had launched his own "Little New Deal," after taking office in January 1935. Democratic Senator Joe Guffey seated between FDR and Earle. Credit: Courtesy of the Pennsylvania State Archives

Governor George H. Earle III meets with striking anthracite coal miners near Coaldale, PA, October 11, 1937. Credit: Image donated to ExplorePAHistory.com by Corbis - Bettmann

**Black Democratic Party Leaders
of Philadelphia, with Governor George Earle.**

**Standing: Samuel Holmes,
J. Austin Norris, and Rev. Marshall Lorenzo Shepard.**

**Sitting: Merce Lewis, Governor Earle,
and Crystal Bird Fauset, March 1940.**

Source: Charles Blockson Collection, Temple University Libraries

Chapter 6

Sofia, Bulgaria

In January 1939, the editorial pages of the *Philadelphia Inquirer* – no friend to George Earle – commented on the governor's dignified departure from office and transition back to civilian life. John M. Cummings, the newspaper's "Strictly Politics" editor wrote the following about the departure of Earle:

> This department, on occasion, has disagreed mildly with some of Mr. Earle's policies as a public official. Socially, however, our relations were never under the slightest strain and on more than one occasion we enjoyed open-handed hospitality. George Earle retiring from office has our best wishes for future success.
>
> We don't know what George Earle will do when he becomes Citizen Earle. There has been some talk of his taking a portfolio under the Great White Father at Washington. He was in the diplomatic service before assuming the Governorship and it may well be he will return to that line of activity …
>
> There was a time when his worship was among those mentioned when politicians fell to speculating on the choice of next year's Democratic national convention.[77]

George Earle was no longer governor, but he desired to continue public service with a return to an ambassadorial position on behalf of FDR. As the *Philadelphia Inquirer* noted separately, his life-long friend, Ambassador Bill Bullitt, seems to have been engaged to lobby for an appointment for Earle. Press reports openly speculated on possible diplomatic postings: Ireland and Canada among the ones most often mentioned. One wonders if Earle himself wasn't "advertising" his preferences through unsourced "news" reports about where he was headed.

Months passed without an ambassadorial appointment. Pennsylvania Democratic Senator Joseph F. Guffey weighed-in for Earle's diplomatic posting abroad. Guffey was probably quite pleased to get Earle a patronage position and politically out of the way, as some Democrats within the Pennsylvania political scene were encouraging Earle to make a run for the Senate and unseat Guffey as the long-time state political boss. Earle's ambassadorial posting would be a "win-win."

In the meanwhile, George Earle continued managing his substantial business interests, circulated in the Main Line social circuit and kept a keen eye on political developments, both domestic and foreign. In late September 1939, Earle penned a commentary for *The Philadelphia Inquirer*, "Who Will Win the War?"[78] A couple of Earle's observations and predictions are stunningly accurate, especially since Europe had only been at war for a couple of weeks, and the Japanese attack on Pearl Harbor was still two years in the future. Among Earle's insights:

> 2. What effect will there be from Russia's treaty with Germany and Russia's invasion of Poland?

> Answer: My first reaction was that these developments were almost fatal to the cause of England and France, because of enabling Germany to fight on one front only, and because of their influence on the Balkan states. A more careful analysis, based on the realization of the racial antipathy of Slav for Teuton, and the long nourished hatred of Nazi for Communist, makes me believe that Germany may have made an alliance with her Frankenstein.

And,

The chances are nine out of ten that London, Berlin, Paris and all the great cities will be, eventually, a mass of ruins.[79]

In an interview syndicated through the *International News Service* on November 3, 1939, Earle proposed the creation of an American "Maginot Line" 500-miles off the coast of the United States, emphasizing use of US naval and air power. Earle cautioned against, "a quiet move by an expanding militaristic foreign power to gain a foothold in South or Central America . . . patterned after Germany's coups in the Sudetenland and Danzig."[80]

The infamous "Zimmerman Telegram"[iii] of World War I, combined with Hitler's aggressive moves to "protect German ethnic groups" seem to have been the inspiration for Earle's thinking. He specifically cited Germany, Japan and Russia as sources of potential danger to the Western Hemisphere and the United States.

By late January 1940, Earle and Guffey were meeting with FDR in the White House to discuss a foreign post.[81] Earle's earlier duties as Minister to Austria helped frame his next assignment. The Balkans were a tinderbox of uncertainty for US foreign policy. Since European hostilities commenced in September 1939, the situation in the Balkans (the flashpoint for World War I) had been "in play" – caught between the pressures of Nazi Germany, historical Slav attachment to the Russian (now Soviet) government and the uneasy neutrality of Turkey. George Earle had firsthand insights and contacts in the region from his days in Vienna. In short order, the decision was made – Earle was headed for Sofia, the capital of the Kingdom of Bulgaria.

[iii] The Zimmermann Telegram was a January 1917 secret diplomatic communication issued from the German Foreign Office proposing a military alliance between Germany and Mexico in the event the United States entered World War I against Germany. The telegram was intercepted by British intelligence and outraged the American public. Mexico was promised Texas, New Mexico and Arizona in return for siding with Germany.

NEW ENVOY—Ex-Governor George H. Earle, right, of Pennsylvania, was sworn in yesterday at State Department as Minister to Bulgaria. Witnessing ceremony were Secretary of State Hull and Mrs. Earle. He expects to sail for new post March 9. 82

Earle was sworn-in at the State Department as Minister for the post in Sofia, Bulgaria and the Court of King Boris on February 14, 1940. Bulgaria was the scene for diplomatic maneuvering, intrigue, and espionage – all of which Earle found irresistible. On March 9, 1940 the Earle family (less son, Hubert, who was studying at Harvard) set sail for Europe aboard the *S.S. Washington*. Earle presented his credentials to King Boris on April 2, 1940.

Earle's official portfolio and authority from his friend, FDR, was much broader and deeper than a mere ministerial posting to a small kingdom. Earle's extensive personal travels through Europe and his time as FDR's Minister to Austria – combined with his innate political senses – made him the perfect pick to read the rapidly changing developments in Bulgaria, the Balkans and Central Europe. Earle's first job may have been to keep his friend, King Boris, out of the war – but Earle's contacts and influence from Budapest to Istanbul provided FDR a window into Europe and a source of reporting he was receiving nowhere else. Earle appreciated "geopolitics," the term coined by Swedish political scientist Rudolf Kjellén at the turn of the last century and increasingly coming into vogue during the interwar period. Earle may not have used the word, but his cables to FDR show a deep, nuanced, appreciation for the personalities, politics, geography, cultures, economics and practicalities of life in Europe.

— PITTSBURGH POST-GAZETTE:

Bulgaria's King Boris Greets Diplomats

King Boris, commander-in-chief of Bulgaria's army and chief magistrate of the Order of Bravery, greets a diplomat's wife during the celebration of St. George Victorious day May 6. Army parades mark the day throughout the Balkan country, the most imposing one being in Sofia under the personal guidance of the king. United States Minister George Howard Earle, III, former Pennsylvania governor, and his wife may be seen in center of group.

—Associated Press Photo

83

King Boris was facing increasing pressure from Hitler to side with The Axis. The Bulgarian General Staff also favored the Germans and reflected the historical Bulgarian national anxiety over Russia and Turkey.[84] The leadership of the Bulgarian police and security services also favored their Nazi counterparts, and as we shall see, had a collaborative liaison relationship with the Germans. Adding to the mix, Boris was on very friendly personal terms with both Earle and German Chief of the *Abwehr* Wilhelm Canaris. Much more on the enigmatic Canaris later.

Earle set about his Balkan emissary duties energetically. Within weeks of his arrival in Sofia, he visited Bucharest, Romania and Istanbul, Turkey. Foreign press reports note his travels (perhaps with Earle's encouragement) but contain scant details concerning who he was meeting or the goals of his travels. On May 24, 1940, the *International News Service* reported:

> United States Minster George H. Earle left Sofia for
> Bucharest today for what he described as a trip to obtain
> "personal information."
>
> In view of Earle's visit to Istanbul ten days ago, his new
> trip caused considerable speculation in diplomatic circles.
>
> The Romanian Army was ordered on a full mobilization
> basis yesterday.[85]

Later, on November 14, 1940, the *Associated Press* bureau
in Istanbul issued a short blurb noting, "George H. Earle, US
minister to Bulgaria, arrived here by automobile tonight, expressing
a preference not to discuss the reason for his visit to Turkey."[86]

Earle's political savvy added a public relations dimension to
his diplomatic work. He liked the press and got along personally and
socially with any number of the Balkan beat foreign correspondents,
to include: Bob St. John of the *Associated Press*; Hugo Spaek of the
United Press; Russell Hill of the *New York Herald Tribune*; David
Walker of the *London Daily Mirror* and *Reuters*; Frank Faul of
NBC; George Weller of the *Chicago News*; Cedric Salter of the
Daily Mail; and Michael Padev of the *London Times*. Earle knew
precisely how to "use" the press to accomplish his various missions.
In postwar memoirs, journalists Cedric Salter and Michael Padev
contribute to our understanding of Earle's activities that did not
necessarily make their way into the text of official diplomatic cables
bound for Foggy Bottom.

Traveling from Sofia, Earle ranged further north into
Budapest, Hungary, as well. Like Bulgaria, Hungary were feeling
the Nazi squeeze while struggling to maintain sovereignty. While in
Budapest, Earle met a strikingly beautiful nightclub singer –
Adrienne Molnar – who would later play a role in Earle's Istanbul
intrigues, and in post-war days continue to be of interest to the
British Security Service (MI5) who maintained a substantial file on
her clandestine activities.

Earle's close relationship with King Boris gleaned valuable intelligence for FDR. King Boris and Foreign Minister Popoff faithfully relayed their conversations with Hitler, Ribbentrop and their inner circles, as well as their observations and impressions of Nazi leadership. The Germans had a keen interest in Balkan relations, as the Ploesti oilfields and the nine refineries in the region were a major source of petroleum products for the Reich. The Nazi leadership also sought to influence and manage relations between Hungary, Romania and Bulgaria who were still grappling with boundary and population questions unresolved since the Treaty of Trianon in 1920. The Nazi's feared Soviet intervention and meddling in the region as Central European countries resolved their differences and skated on the thin ice of occupation and alliance.

At some point in 1940, Earle may have had a direct exchange with Hitler, as reported by the Historical Society of Pennsylvania: "A year into his assignment, the former Pennsylvania governor made headlines when he purportedly told Adolf Hitler during a private meeting that 'I have nothing against the Germans, I just don't like you.'"[87]

In September 1940, Earle cabled Washington detailing German and Soviet intentions based on direct reporting from Foreign Minister Popoff and King Boris. Later in the autumn of 1940, Earle's frank reports described a November visit by King Boris and Popoff to Hitler's Berchtesgaden retreat. King Boris told Earle that Hitler wanted peace in the Balkans to ensure Germany's food supply from the region, and that as long as strict neutrality were maintained he did not contemplate military action against Yugoslavia or Turkey. Despite the talk of peace, Earle reported:

> I had one disturbing impression from this interview which if correct may reflect this country's future course. For the first time since I have been here Popoff, probably expressing the feelings of the King, seemed to believe in ultimate German victory.[88]

In addition to his good relations with the Bulgarian Crown, Earle was busy establishing and developing his sources across the political spectrum. A December 1940 cable to the State Department provides important intelligence on Soviet efforts to lure the Bulgarians into an arrangement that would dramatically redraw the map and almost certainly thrust Bulgaria into the war:

> [Sava] Ganovsky, Secretary of the Bulgarian Communist organization (illegal) informs me that [Arkady] Soboleff asked the King for naval and air bases in Bulgaria. Russia in return offered to force Turkey to give Adrianople [Edirne] and Turkish Thrace to Bulgaria and to exert all possible pressure on Greece to cede Grecian Thrace to the Kavala [Aegean seaport] – Drama line. Ganovsky says the King has courteously but firmly refused Russia's proposals.[89]

The Nazi intelligence and security services paid very close attention to Earle. They were keenly aware of his direct access to FDR and for Earle's outspoken, fearless support of Austrian Chancellor Dollfuß while serving as Minister in Austria. Press reports like the ones cited above practically baited the Germans to overplay their hands and put them in a negative light in view of King Boris.

The Battle of the Bottles in the Balkans

The alliterative title for this episode of Earle's term as minister to Bulgaria was coined by an unidentified reporter posing a question to FDR about his emissary's scrappy, physical engagement with Nazi officers in a Sofia nightclub. FDR adopted the catchy phrase with glee in unapologetically defending Earle.

While there are a few versions of the tale detailing the Sofia nightclub "battle," we are fortunate to have a signed legation press release statement from Earle, as well as other corroborative accounts.

Sometime late on the evening of Saturday, February 23, 1941, Minister George H. Earle III, his assistant Marty Meadows, a British intelligence officer and two journalists (Bob St. John and Hugo Spaek) repaired to a Sofia restaurant and nightclub – Maxim's.

By February 1941, many thought an overt invasion of Bulgaria by the Nazis was nearly imminent. German officers, in and out of uniform, treated Sofia as an "R&R" station, frequenting restaurants, bars, theatres and other places of entertainment.

At Maxim's that evening, a table of civilian-attired Nazis took offense when Earle requested the band strike up a rousing rendition of the World War I British marching song, "Tipperary." One of the Germans stood up and ordered the band leader to stop. Maxim's manager reportedly scurried over to Earle and reported that the gentlemen a cross the lounge were Nazis and found the playing of "Tipperary" an insulting provocation against the German army. Earle then summoned the band leader to his table, gave him a substantial tip. The band's playing of "Tipperary" resumed immediately.

The Germans became agitated and began shouting insults and threats to Earle and his companions. Earle decided to make use of the facilities at that point and walked directly towards the German table in route to the men's room. Here we have the benefit of Earle's own signed statement:

> As I passed this German's table he suddenly growled at me: 'What do you mean by ordering the orchestra to play that tune? Don't you realize it is against Germany?'
>
> His face was livid with rage. I tried to hold my temper. I replied as courteously as I could that I liked the tune, that Bulgaria was a neutral country, that I intended to do and say what I please.
>
> His face became contorted with anger. Then he reached for an empty wine bottle on his table. I quickly stepped

back and threw up my hands to protect myself. I was not afraid of being hit, but I have always in polo accidents and plane crackups had a fear of losing my eyesight.

The bottle, which the German threw at close range, struck me on the forearm. A bruise which later appeared was more than six inches long.

This sudden, vicious, unprovoked attack irritated me considerably. I also faced the necessity of defending myself against further vicious attacks, so I smashed him in the face, knocking him down and causing his face to bleed.

My friends at this point suddenly grabbed me and pushed me into a small adjoining room. All Bulgarians present also rallied to my side and helped protect me. The German was joined by a great many other Germans in civilian clothes who rushed to his side from various parts of the restaurant. They made many attempts to charge through the wall of Bulgarians standing in front of me, but each time without success.

It was one hour later that order finally was reestablished enough so we could leave the restaurant and go to the American legation.[90]

Michael Padev, a Bulgarian journalist and graduate of the American College in Sofia recounts a few additional details about the skirmish, having been summoned to the American Legation in the early morning hours of Sunday, February 24th in order to hear Earle's side of things in the company of other sympathetic journalists. Upon arriving at the legation, Padev witnessed, "Earle looked as though he had just taken a shower and had forgotten to take off his clothes first. His trousers were sopping. His shirt was torn and had slipped off one shoulder and on that shoulder a large dark bruise was embossed."[91]

We learn from Padev that the Bulgarians rushing to reinforce the Earle position at Maxim's were taxi drivers who had been summoned from their rank across the road by one of Maxim's waiters. Purportedly, the taxi drivers all knew Earle and his journalist friends as loyal customers and big tippers. Padev notes that, "they [taxi drivers] took to the fray with great gusto."[92]

Earle's "Battle of the Bottles" was a press sensation on both sides of the Atlantic. In the United States, some senators and political pundits called for his immediate recall and dismissal from ambassadorial rank. The career State Department striped-pants set at Foggy Bottom were mortified. The *Los Angeles Times* ran the headline, "Nazi Beaten by Earle, Envoy, Reported Dying," reporting:

> Officials of the United States Legation tonight said they are trying to track down repeated report that a German injured by Minister George H. Earle is dying of a fractured skull. A check of hotels and hospitals failed to disclose any trace of the man . . .

> Earle himself said he had received one report that the man was dying of a skull fracture. He said the best information he had been able to obtain was that the man was a member of the German general staff.

> He said that 'one of the officers who had recently filtered from Rumania into Bulgaria in civilian clothes' had been shipped by German officials back to Bucharest. Earle added that the German Legation had declined to disclose the man's name and was 'maintaining strange secrecy.'

> The official German news agency, D.N.B., issued a version of the affair in which it said Earle was responsible for the fight and charged that this was Earle's 'fourth barroom brawl' in the Balkans.

> The news agency did not elaborate this point but some months ago Earle and a German engaged in a scuffle on the dance floor at Budapest's famed Arizona Night Club and the management telephoned officials of the American Legation at the Hungarian capital.

Once before Earle tangled with a German at Sofia, at the Etoile Night Club, and Earle said he had been informed by Bulgarian officials that police investigation disclosed 'I was a victim of unwanted aggression in which I was in no way to blame and that I had been exonerated from all responsibility.'

The former Governor of Pennsylvania suffered a forearm bruise in yesterday's altercation. He confined himself to his office, in which he keeps a tame leopard, and to his home. He said he had taken special steps to protect himself.[93]

Others cheered Earle and congratulated him for being the first American to draw blood against the Nazis. A group of Pennsylvania judges sent Earle commendations, "Congratulations on live spunk and dead aim," radiogramed Judges John H. McGann, Charles C. Greer, I.J. McKenrick, and A.A. Nelson.[94]

The Nazi press branded Earle an enemy and a criminal. The German magazine, *Illustrierte Zeitung*, ran a series of articles ranking Earle as the number one enemy of the Nazis in the Balkans.[95]

Dr. Karl Becker, whom the *United Press* described as a "German industrialist" came forward on February 27 and asserted that Earle had called him a "damned Nazi," and struck the first blow without provocation. Dr. Becker reportedly filed a legal complaint against Earle in an effort to make his side of the brawl known. The legal complaint came to no affect, but the semi-official German foreign office publication, *Diplomatisch Politische Korrespondenz* declared Earle a "boorish, cowardly liar."[96]

Meanwhile, back in Haverford, local Pennsylvania press interviewed Mrs. Earle concerning her husband's Bulgarian adventures. She noted for the interviewer that, "George always craved excitement."[97]

Mrs. Earle went on to describe her time in Sofia before being evacuated back to the United States: "In spite of the blackouts there was a great deal of festivity and party-going in Sofia, which, incidentally, happens to be a very beautiful, gay and sophisticated city." She explained that the U.S. Legation building had first been offered to the French, but because it faced the rear end of an equestrian statue of Tsar Alexander II of Russia, the French refused it on a point of national pride. Apparently, Minister Earle had no such esthetic sensitivities.[98]

Maxim's resembled "Rick's Café Américain" in the 1943 film classic *Casablanca*, staring Humphrey Bogart, Ingrid Bergman and Claude Raines, among others. Maxim's figures in the tale of Earle's relationship with a beautiful Hungarian nightclub singer and dancer, Adrienne Molnar, who we will discuss at length in the context of Earle's duties in Istanbul and his work against the Abwehr. Maxim's was also the Sofia night spot was where the chief of the Office of Strategic Services (OSS – the precursor of the Central Intelligence Agency), Colonel "Wild Bill" Donovan, had his wallet lifted by persons unknown. This came only two weeks following Earle's "battle." Colonel Donovan's wallet was "found" by the Bulgarian police a few days later and returned to Minister Earle. Colonel Donovan toured the Balkans in March 1941 for FDR.

The Bulgarian journalist Padev recounts in his memoir that the German's were highly suspicious of Earle's activities across the Balkans and Central Europe, and assigned special importance to Donovan's visit to Sofia. Padev was arrested in the late Spring of 1941 and interrogated by Herr Julius Drexler of the *Geheime Staatspolizei*, Gestapo, or Nazi Secret State Police. Drexler quizzed Padev repeatedly concerning the nature and frequency of his contacts with Earle, at one point accusing Padev of being an agent of Earle's. The Donovan visit was also of great interest to Drexler. Padev explained his contacts with the American Legation as a journalist, "I explained this to Drexler but it did not satisfy him. He attacked Earle in the most violent terms. 'He, too, belongs to the Secret Service!' he screamed. 'We know all about his nefarious activities in Vienna. He acted then as a liaison between Dollfuß and the White House and now he's running all the American spy organizations in the Balkans.'[99]

Wild Bill Donovan Has a Look in Bulgaria

President Roosevelt's personal representative, Col. William J. Donovan, center, inspects a military school in Sofia, Bulgarian capital, in company of George Earle, U. S. minister, and General Ninoff, head of the school. This is one of the first pictures of Earle to arrive in America since the former Pennsylvania governor's champagne-bottle imbroglio with Germans in a Sofia night club. [100]

Earle recovered quickly from his fight at Maxim's, and by early March was testing the limits of his diplomatic status and the growing Nazi dominance over Bulgaria. He made a trek by automobile with a group of American journalists to Bulgaria's border with Yugoslavia, where the Bulgarian authorities refused to allow him to cross the border. The border confrontation and brief detention made headlines – pointing out the precarious position Bulgaria found itself under growing Nazi pressure and imminent military occupation.[101]

Concurrent with Earle's border expedition, Secretary of State Cordell Hull announced the U.S. government would freeze Bulgaria's credits and balances in the United States as soon as German troops occupied the country. Bulgaria's gold reserves as of

1939 totaled approximately $24,000,000.[102] Bulgaria begrudgingly signed-on to the Tripartite Pact on March 1, 1941. Clearly, the move towards war mounted with each passing day.

Following the fight at Maxim's, the visit of Colonel Donovan and the border detention incident, things continued to heat-up for Earle as U.S. Minister. He faced a number of death threats, a Nazi inspired march on the Legation by Bulgarian citizens, telephone tapping and tampering with his automobile in a manner suggesting that an attempt to rig explosives had been interrupted.

Speaking to the Philadelphia chapter of the Military Order of the World War in February 1942, Earle recounted how the American flag on his ministerial automobile precipitated an incident with German soldiers one evening in Sofia:

> One of the soldiers, speaking perfect English, asked if I was an American," Earle said. "When I told him I was, he said: 'You don't like us Nazis, do you,' and I told him I did not.
>
> I started to get into my car and one of the soldiers grabbed me by the leg and tried to pull me out. I kicked him with all my might in the stomach and one of the other two soldiers took a punch at me that would have been a haymaker had it landed. As it was, the first brushed my nose.
>
> I gave him a straight left to the jaw, got the car going and sped down the street, where I turned around and headed back, seeking to run down the three Nazis.
>
> I chased them up on the sidewalk with my small car. They got in a doorway and I couldn't get at them, so I drove home. People on the street laughed in amusement at the undignified positions of the soldiers.[103]

A Gestapo officer named Beckerle recruited a White Russian refugee named Alexis Borissevitch to penetrate the U.S. Legation and spy on Earle. The Russian was in a vulnerable position as a stateless person living with a "Nansen passport" – a League of Nations identity document that placed his refugee status in the hands of the Nazi-controlled Bulgarian police. Alexis was employed as a messenger for the U.S. Legation.

Beckerle, through his Bulgarian police associates, Chief Pavel Pavlov and his counterintelligence assistant, Prometaroff, directed Alexis to steal and photograph U.S. documents, and to gain access to the legation code room, where diplomatic cables were prepared, transmitted and received. The plot failed. Earle and his assistant, Marty Meadows, became suspicious of Alexis and in short order confronted him about his nervous, suspicious conduct. Alexis confessed the plot. Earle quickly arrived at his own course of action to protect the legation and Alexis. He ordered a staff member to sleep in the secured code room; generated a U.S. passport for Alexis to flee Bulgaria; and, met directly with King Boris to apprise him of the plot.[104]

Six days following the Japanese attack on Pearl Harbor – on the afternoon of Saturday, December 13th – a mob of at least 300 Bulgarian youths armed with rocks, bricks and sticks descended on the American Legation. Bulgaria and America were officially now at war, and George Earle was returning to his place of pride at the front line of confrontation. The mob turned violent and proceeded to smash every window in the legation, that also served as Earle's diplomatic residence. Prepared to fight fire with fire, Earle retrieved his Winchester lever-action rifle and moved towards the now-smashed windows. Apparently, Earle was prepared to open fire on the mob – or perhaps, he intended to fire warning shots – or even simply brandish the weapon before the mob as a deterrence. We will never know what might have happened, as Earle was wrestled to the floor by two legation staff who were terrified of what the minister might provoke by some form of armed response.[105]

Mounted police units eventually subdued and dispersed the crowd. Shortly before midnight, King Boris paid a visit to the legation and his dear friend, George Earle. King Boris told Earle, "I am surprised, but I am relieved to see you alive."[106]

War came to Bulgaria, so Earle and much of his staff left by train for Istanbul. King Boris feared a Nazi plot to murder Earle in the confusion and commotion of the entry of Field Marshal List's German troops as occupiers. Earle arrived in Istanbul on December 27, 1941, in the private car of King Boris, escorted by His Majesty's private secretary.

International press coverage of Earle's arrival in Istanbul was extensive, but the German press took a particularly nasty line on Earle, seeking to portray his arrival in decadently sensational, almost cartoonish style. The German news agency purported that Earle, "had thirty-eight pieces of luggage, bags and boxes contained over a hundred bottles of toilet water, distilled especially for him from Bulgaria's fragrant rose petals, and an enormous collection of jeweled cigarette cases, old gold coins, antique icons and other church artifacts. Although he had to leave behind 'Pussy,' a tamed cheetah, he and brought his three dachshunds and another kind of a pet, a willowy blonde the German reporter identified as 'a Jewish cabaret dancer named Adrienne.'"[107] The German article was deliberately reckless and insulting. A hit piece. Earle had been at the top of the Nazis' blacklist since his days in Vienna, and they were growing increasingly wary of him.

"Adrienne" was Adrienne Molnar, a Hungarian nightclub singer whom Earle had met in Budapest at some point during his diplomatic travels while based in Sofia. Theirs was an on-and-off relationship complicated by distance, war, and espionage. When Earle eventually returned to Istanbul as Naval Attaché, approximately a year after his royal train evacuation from Sofia, he would seek out Adrienne in Budapest (where she had returned) and arrange for her to join him. She would feature significantly in the wartime Istanbul espionage milieu, and as an intelligence operative for several years afterwards.

Adrienne Molnar, 1941. MI5 security files, UK National Archives

After a few weeks in Istanbul, Earle returned to the United States on January 29, 1942. He was greeted upon his arrival at the North Philadelphia train station by his wife, Huberta, whom he had not seen in more than two years, and a group of approximately 30 friends and family. The six-day trip included a route aboard an Army Air Corps bomber from Cairo, across North Africa, to South America, then north to an unspecified Caribbean island where he caught a Pan Am Clipper flying to New York. Accompanying him to New York and Philadelphia was William C. Bullitt, his old friend and FDR's special envoy to the Near East, who had just completed a tour of the region. Earle was his ebullient self on the train platform, granting an impromptu press conference. He traced his journey, pointing out two near-death plane incidents. Earle also made a point of setting aside further political ambitions "for the duration," and stated his desire to return to commissioned service in the US Navy.[108]

On May 9, 1942, Lieutenant Commander (LCDR) Earle reported for duty aboard the *USS Hermitage*, a troop transport originally launched in 1925 from a Scottish shipyard for service as the Italian liner *SS Conte Biancamano*. With the entry of the United States into the war, she was seized from the Panamanian port of Cristóbal and converted to carry approximately 7,000 men. The ship was armed with only one 5"/38mm gun and six 3"/50mm guns for anti-aircraft protection. Fifty-two year old LCDR Earle, who had last seen active Naval duty in 1919, was the gunnery officer of the *USS Hermitage*. The *Hermitage* departed New York on November 2, 1942 for the invasion of North Africa, codenamed "Operation Torch."[109]

Ever resourceful and energetic, the *Hermitage's* new gunnery officer set about to improve the air defenses of the troop ship. Earle's official US Navy record, obtained from the National Personnel Records Center, contains a two-page citation, dated November 18, 1942, endorsed by two US Army colonels and approved by the *Hermitage's* Captain, A.D. Douglas, for Earle's "superior initiative, foresight, and cooperation which resulted in providing the Hermitage with the most effective anti-aircraft protection possible."[110] Somehow, Earle had managed to add six 40mm Bofors guns, and four 50-caliber machine guns to the *Hermitage*. The record is not clear as to exactly how he accomplished it. He also trained and drilled 140 soldiers and crew to supplement anti-aircraft gun fire with M1 rifle fire.

The *Hermitage* debarked troops at Casablanca beginning November 18, 1942 for the North Africa Campaign. It was in Casablanca where Earle would encounter an old friend: Major General George S. Patton.

Amusingly, the State Department still had unresolved business with the former Minister to Bulgaria. Earle, through his unconventional diplomatic style, seems to have left an impression on the career foreign service establishment. They managed to track down LCDR Earle in Morocco with a "Note of Indebtedness" from the Consulate General in Beirut, which was routed through the Chief of Naval Personnel with four endorsements, seeking payment of $22.94 for expenses incurred transporting Earle's Hungarian shepherd dog, "Muki," from Sofia to Philadelphia. Earle paid the bill by money order on December 18, 1942.

Chapter 7

Casablanca

Earle spent approximately two weeks in Casablanca as the men and materiel of the *Hermitage* unloaded and the ship refitted for its return to the United States. He spent much of his time with a fellow polo player and friend, George S. Patton. We know this thanks to a December 18, 1942 note from FDR to Mr. Fred Shipman, FDR's archivist. FDR's note discusses a report and photographs from Patton on his first days in French Morocco, that had been hand-delivered to FDR by Earle on December 14, 1942.[111]

FDR's note reads:

THE WHITE HOUSE
WASHINGTON
December 18, 1942

MEMORANDUM FOR MR. SHIPMAN

This report must be kept secret until after the close of the war. It is by Major General Patton who commanded the Cavalry at Fort Meyer soon after I came to Washington. He was one of the earliest Cavalry officers to shift to tanks. He came to see me at the White House two weeks before the American Expedition started for Casablanca and I asked him whether he had his old Cavalry saddle to mount on the turret of a tank and if he went into action on the side with his saber drawn. Patton is a joy and this report of his first days in French Morocco is a classis [sic].

The report and the accompanying photographs were brought to me on December fourteenth by Lt. Commander George Earle, Gunnery Officer of the USS

HERMITAGE, who is an old friend of Patton and had spent several days ashore with him at Casablanca.

F. D. R.

The 10-pages of single-spaced reporting from Patton is colorful, brutally frank and highly entertaining. The report is in two parts and contains both a summary of various events (one believes Earle witnessed in large part) soon after the American landings, and a copy of Patton's letter to the Sultan of Morocco. The photos feature Patton meeting the Moroccan Prince, the Grand Vizier, and the Sultan.

During Earle's December 14th meeting with FDR, it appears he lobbied for reassignment from troop transport gunnery duty to something more consistent with his substantial ambassadorial and executive experience. While the immediate wartime "needs of the naval service" may have initially placed Earle aboard a troop transport as a gunnery officer, that decision was clearly not in the best interests of the country, the FDR administration, nor Earle.

Just months earlier, Earle had been FDR's eyes and ears in the Balkans and Central Europe. He had an extensive network of contacts in Berlin, Warsaw, Vienna, Budapest, Bucharest, Athens, Istanbul, and, of course, Sofia. Varying theories and loosely sourced intelligence of anti-Hitler and German resistance plotting had reached Washington via OSS representatives in Europe. A frequent locus of conspiracy in the reporting was Istanbul. Earle had the experience, area knowledge and contacts. He had direct access to and moved freely in circles career State Department officials either dreamed about or were terrified of contemplating. He was independently wealthy and could act without waiting for a cable from Washington authorizing an expenditure of funds. These facts made him extraordinarily effective and very unpopular at Foggy Bottom. A State Department posting was not feasible, but there was another option.

So it is not surprising that following his meeting with his old friend FDR on December 14th, orders were issued from the Chief of Naval Operations on December 29, 1942 reassigning LCDR Earle from the *USS Hermitage* to report to the Vice Chief of Naval Operations for temporary duty in route to assignment as the "Assistant Naval Attaché and Assistant Naval Attaché for Air," American Embassy, Turkey "in connection with specific Lend-Lease activities and certain post-war food problems."[112] That was an extraordinarily thin diplomatic cover, but diplomatic cover nonetheless. Handwritten file notes indicate the telephonic order from the White House to the Navy occurred on December 18th.

George H. Earle III was now FDR's personal emissary. Earle traveled with FDR to Casablanca in January 1943, then continued on to his assignment in Turkey.[113]

In January 1943, FDR and Churchill met in Casablanca, Morocco. Two months following the successful execution of Operation Torch, the invasion of North Africa, the leaders focused on the next strategic step for the western allies. The Sicily-Italy Campaign dominated conference discussions.

Overshadowing any other communique of the conference was the seemingly spontaneous announcement by FDR that the allies would accept only "unconditional surrender" of the Axis. The announcement surprised Churchill, FDR's staff and the flag officers present. What may have been intended as "tough talk," wartime jingoism, or a salve to Premier Stalin, who did not attend the conference citing the ongoing Battle of Stalingrad, foreclosed any chance for a negotiated end to the war. The consequences for FDR's seemingly off-the-cuff ultimatum were grave.

Hanson W. Baldwin, the military editor of the *New York Times*, analyzed the effects of FDR's ultimatum in his 1950 book, "Great Mistakes of the War." Baldwin's view was that FDR had made an "open invitation to unconditional resistance; it discouraged opposition to Hitler; probably lengthened the war, cost us lives, and helped to lead to the present abortive peace ..."[114]

The term "unconditional surrender" was not lost on the Nazi government, and perhaps more importantly, on the German military. German generals were now backed into a corner. One constraining wall for the professional German officer corps was Duty, the other was Honor. Whatever illusions the German officer corps maintained about a negotiated armistice on the Western Front as a measure to buy time and space for defeating what they viewed as the "real enemy" – Soviet Bolshevism – were shattered.

British historian B. H. Liddell Hart interviewed a number of German general officers following the war. He published those interviews in 1948. The consensus view was, "All to whom I talked dwelt on the effect of the Allies' "unconditional surrender" policy in prolonging the war. They told me that but for this they and their troops – the factor that was more important – would have been ready to surrender sooner, separately, or collectively ..."[115]

FDR's demand for "unconditional surrender" would launch Earle on a mission of clandestine intrigue. It is probable that neither FDR nor his old friend, Earle, imagined in the moment the broad consequences or the personal jeopardy one seemingly cavalier presidential quip would entail.

In January 1943, the Stalingrad encirclement was nearly complete. Within a month the German Sixth Army would be compelled to surrender. The Nazi leadership comprehended this momentous shift in the tide of the war. This was the period for an opening in the window for the German resistance and the Allies to arrive at an armistice and remove Hitler under terms other than "unconditional surrender."[116]

Chapter 8

Istanbul

Earle's presence in Istanbul is the hinge point of an untold, suppressed history. All that transpired concerning the approach by German resistance leaders for an armistice and uncovering the truth of the Katyn Forest massacre could only have happened in Istanbul. The neutral status of Turkey; the foreign diplomatic missions; intelligence officers and their front operations; the bustling port; the city's unique geography; restaurants, casinos, hotels and nightclubs; refugees, expatriate aristocrats, artists, writers and revolutionaries; even the smugglers and forgers of the city's criminal underground, all were tiles in a unique mosaic of intrigue.

The Turks walked a tightrope of technical neutrality between Berlin and Moscow, while secretly cooperating with the Americans and British, in the hope the latter countries would eventually save them from the pressure and intrigues of the former. There were provocations. The Soviets attempted to kill German Ambassador Franz von Papen in a bomb plot meant to frame Turkish actors and provoke war with Germany. The British had attempted to lure Turkish President Ismet Inönü (who held the honorific title, "Millî Sef" [National Chief] as successor to Kemal Atatürk) to their side by dispatching an expeditionary force to Greece as the Germans moved south through the Balkans into Bulgaria. All sides offered Inönü land, and "border adjustments" for basing rights, port access and free transit. Inönü's private reaction to all of these pressures was, "I am not Enver Pasha [Ottoman Empire leader during World War I], they cannot drag me into a war."[117]

Istanbul, the bridge between Europe and Asia, crossroads of empires and civilizations, an eclectic mix of the ancient and modern, hub of commerce, and in 1943, a neutral city where intelligence officers of all the warring states, various revolutionary and underground operatives, as well as freelance characters with their own interests, might all be seated at tables scattered about the Taksim Kasino, the restaurants at the Park Hotel or the Tokatlıyan, or any other of the city's night spots on any given evening.

Earle's assignment to Turkey as FDR's personal emissary apparently struck a nerve, again, at the State Department. Secretary of State Hull sent a personal cable to the American Embassy in Ankara announcing Earle's appointment as "Assistant Naval Attaché" and detailing Earle's date of rank for protocol purposes. There was no mention of him having been an Ambassador, twice. No reference to his status as personal emissary of the President. The key notation: "It seems that Gov. Earle is to arrive in Ankara in a few days. It is essential that the Ambassador be informed in advance of his arrival."[118] After reporting in at the American Embassy in Ankara, Earle took up residence in a large, luxurious suite in the Park Hotel, with views of the Bosporus. It was January 23, 1943.

Lieutenant Commander George H. Earle III, U.S.N.R.
Assistant U.S. Naval Attaché, Istanbul, 1943
Courtesy of Melanie Earle Lynagh

Enter Adrienne Molnar. The beautiful Hungarian night club singer was living in Budapest. Earle wanted her to join him in Istanbul. It had been a year since they had seen each other, on the occasion of Earle's departure from Sofia to Istanbul, aboard the private train car of King Boris. Ever skirting the rules, the "Assistant US Naval Attaché" sent a personal telegram from neutral Istanbul to Hungary (a country nominally at war with the United States). Historian Ladislas Farago reports Earle's wire was addressed:

> to Miss Adrienne Molnar, at 12 Muskatli Utca, a street in Budapest whose name was aptly romantic under the circumstances. "Muskatli" means geranium and the wire was intended to revive a flowering friendship which the war had rudely interrupted. Signed "Hefty," the pet name by which Adrienne called George, the message was in Hungarian; an English text would have complicated things for Miss Molnar. It advised her that he was staying

in the Park Hotel, where he expected her arrival at her earliest convenience.[119]

Farago is, of course, the Hungarian-born military historian and acclaimed biographer of General George S. Patton, whose *"Patton: Ordeal and Triumph,"* was the basis for the film, "Patton." He wrote extensively on espionage during the World War II era, and was renowned for his personal interviews, investigations, and access to previously classified information, to include German, French and Argentinian records. Before the war, he was a journalist covering Europe and the Middle East. During the war, he was with the Office of Naval Intelligence in Washington, DC. His research and writing, featured principally in his book *"The Game of the Foxes,"* is important to understand the German intrigues targeting Earle.

Adrienne Molnar had come to the attention of the German intelligence services through her romantic relationship with Earle. She was featured in German press reports on Earle's arrival via royal Bulgarian train car in Istanbul as the "Jewish cabaret dancer." Earle's cable to Adrienne in Budapest also did not escape German attention.

Excited by Earle's cable to join him in Istanbul, Adrienne had a problem. She did not have a visa permitting her to leave Hungary nor to enter Turkey. As fate would have it, Adrienne had a dear friend, a sort of "aunt" or confidante in the person of Frau Asta Matzhold, the wife of Louis Matzhold, an Austrian journalist who had been posted in Washington, and was now reporting from Budapest for the *Berliner Boersen-Zeitung*, an economics daily styled after the *Wall Street Journal*.[120]

Adrienne may, or may not have known at that time was that Louis Matzhold was a sort of free-lance German intelligence operative, most closely associated with the *Abwehr*, the German military intelligence agency headed by Admiral Wilhelm Canaris. Operating under the codename "Michael," Matzhold had reported from Washington DC since at least 1937. Canaris distrusted the use of journalists as intelligence officers and required Matzhold's affiliation to the *Abwehr* be termed as a "*Gewaersmann*" – literally, "business man." Matzhold was a free-lancer or a stringer, sending long reports to Berlin claiming inside information from important Washington contacts in government. Matzhold's most potent claim: that he had an "intimate relationship" with FDR over their shared love of stamp-collecting, and that he would visit FDR on Saturday evenings discussing all things philatelic and not. There is no documentation in the National Archives or the Roosevelt Library at Hyde Park, NY detailing visits by Matzhold. That does not mean that Matzhold was exaggerating or lying, as FDR was certainly secretive and not all private visitors were recorded in diaries and calendars.[121]

Likewise, the British have almost no records on Louis Matzhold, other than a name trace request from a Captain Butler of MI5, dated February 9, 1940, "with a view towards ascertaining reliability."[122] The reply to the trace: "Nothing recorded against."

Asta having told her husband of Adrienne's telegram and visa predicament in seeking to rejoin "Hefty" in Istanbul, Matzhold instantly comprehended an opportunity. At this point in his espionage career, Matzhold was still a free-lancer, exercising contacts and opportunities with the *Abwehr*, the *Sicherheitsdeinst* and the intelligence bureau of the German foreign ministry, headed by a friend of Minister Ribbentrop named Rudolph Likus. Matzhold sketched out a concept to Likus for leveraging Adrienne against Earle. It was intriguing enough for Likus to fly from Berlin to Budapest to coordinate with Matzhold. Matzhold, having known Earle since his assignment in the US, would approach Earle as a concerned, helpful friend of Adrienne and a sympathetic, secret, anti-Nazi and anti-Soviet. He would get Adrienne out of Budapest and into Earle's arms, while cementing a confidential relationship with FDR's personal emissary.[123]

Earle apparently saw through Matzhold's ploy immediately, but strung him along to both get Adrienne out of Budapest and feed tantalizing disinformation to the Germans. While Minister to Bulgaria, Earle had met Matzhold twice on fishing trips. He held the "journalist" as useful, but not particularly intelligent. In the course of their wide-ranging conversation on February 4, 1943, Earle told Matzhold that the Allies were planning to land troops in 34 locations when the invasion of Europe took place. Matzhold bolted from the meeting directly to Berlin to report what he believed to be a gold mine of information. The false information given by Earle to Matzhold misled the Germans into diverting troops elsewhere during the Allied invasion of Sicily on July 10, 1943.[124]

Earle's arrival in Istanbul did not escape the attention of the German press. A cable from Leland Harrison, the US Minister in Berne, Switzerland to State Department headquarters, dated February 2, 1943, reports on a German publication from January 29:

> . . . under the headline "Uncle George is back" comment on alleged assignment George Earle as Naval Attaché to Turkey stating his residence in Istanbul should soon inspire scandalous stories and describing his arrival Istanbul year ago from Sofia 'surrounded by several pedigree dogs and number ladies theretofore occupying firmly defined position Sofia nightlife and accompanied by 38 trunks containing 220 thousand dollars' worth jeweled cigarette cases gold and silver coins and ikons acquired basis diplomatic privileges' article then seeks portray Earle as well known to procurers, nightclub singers and Jewish dancers as Uncle George and embroiders incident concerning Colonel Donovan's briefcase adding painful questions House Representatives caused President keep Earle in reserve for further missions in southeastern Europe. Purpose article revealed as effort discredit Earle's assignment by concluding

statement his new diplomatic post is screen fully justifies intrigues against Bulgaria and other Balkan countries also endeavor to discredit character in general of the United States representatives abroad. Repeated to Ankara. HARRISON[125] (sic)

Harrison, like his nominal "assistant" (for cover purposes), Berne OSS Station Chief Allen Dulles, were, at "Hitler's Doorstep" (the title of Dulles' book) and credited by the Germans with being, "particularly well-informed on the situation in Munich, for instance on the morale of the people and on rifts between various High Party officials, between Goering and Himmler, Ribbentrop and Himmler, etc."[126]

Harrison's cable is another example of the State Department's sensitivities regarding Earle. It seems enemy propaganda pieces had the desired effect on career US foreign service officers too. Harrison made sure the American Embassy in Ankara received his report.

Historical opinion on Earle is split. There are favorable and unfavorable commentaries concerning the man, the politician, the diplomat, and, of course, as FDR's personal emissary to the Balkan region. Generally speaking, the career, professional, government establishment-types loathed Earle. They viewed him as a wealthy, privileged, politically-connected amateur. The State Department and his "espionage competitors" at OSS stations across Europe seem solidly in that camp. How dare he? Who does he think he is? By what right does he do the things that he does? Certainly, a good degree of that was petty jealousy over the ability to routinely communicate directly with the President on friendly terms. That is a question of access. Another facet is Earle's wealth. In that case, there may have been some class-envy, combined with Earle's total disregard for budgeting, authorized expenditures, seeking approval for operations and activities, etc. To help understand Earle in this context, two quotes are useful. One from a journalist and another from a German *Abwehr* officer in Istanbul working against Earle.

"Perhaps indiscreet and certainly unorthodox," wrote Cy Sulzberger of *The New York Times*, "Earle was nevertheless a true friend, quite fearless and a gay companion."

The *Abwehr* station chief in Istanbul, Dr. Paul Leverkuehn, wrote the following dispatch to Ambassador von Papen and his *Abwehr* superiors in May 1943:

> Opinions [that Earle was a dilettante] have changed in the British and American embassies about George Earle. It is reported that he has succeeded in reaching an agreement between the United States and Bulgaria. The negotiations took place in Istanbul but mainly through men of Earle's in Sofia. The basis for the agreement is that it should be recognized that Bulgaria has acted under compulsion in her present policy and will return to full neutrality as soon as such compulsion no longer exists. Bulgaria would evacuate all Greek territory that she has occupied. The American Military Attaché says that this agreement is due entirely to the skill of Earle, who has been in direct contact with Roosevelt. A letter from the President to "My dear George," has caused a stir in the American Embassy. It has not yet been decided who will sign for Bulgaria – the King and his government are hesitating and casting about for a suitable person. There are similar reports about Rumania.[127]

As Earle arrived on station in Istanbul, he was being assessed – by Americans and foreigners, friends and foe alike.

Adrienne would eventually arrive in Istanbul aboard the Orient Express in April, with visas facilitated in Hungary and Turkey by the Germans. In the interim, Matzhold and Earle had a couple of additional semi-clandestine meetings. An exhibit of the German's keen interest in Earle's status as presidential emissary was an envelope of purportedly rare postage stamps from German occupied territories that Likus had obtained from the *Abwehr* for

Matzhold to give to Earle – with the idea that he would pass them along to FDR. Earle did so via diplomatic pouch to FDR. One can imagine the president opening an envelope of official *Abwehr* stationary bearing the handwritten notation: "Property of Louis A. Matzhold for the Mister President of the United States." FDR reportedly thanked Matzhold via Earle, but asked that he not use *Abwehr* envelopes in any further communication.[128]

Having fed the Germans with disinformation and secured the release of his girlfriend, Earle cut Matzhold loose, terminating the German's dreamed-of penetration of the presidential emissary's operation in the neutral city. It was a masterstroke of manipulation and hardball tradecraft. Earle told Matzhold that the Russians had bugged his hotel room and recorded their ant-Hitler and anti-Soviet discussions. He purportedly knew this thanks to a friendly visit from the British MI6 officer (and former *New York Times* correspondent) George Gedye, who had somehow managed to get ahold of the recordings. How this turn of events came about lacks a clear explanation, but it was sufficient for Matzhold to break direct contact with Earle and now rely upon "access agent," Adrienne Molnar.[129]

In love as in war, things do not necessarily go as planned. Just a few days before Adrienne was set to board the Orient Express and reunite with "Hefty," he telegrammed her, asking that she stay in Budapest and that he would provide for her. It is not clear if this was a personal change of heart, an effort to insulate Adrienne from manipulation and possible harm from the Nazis, or something else. Nonetheless, Adrienne arrived in Istanbul and Earle was overjoyed to see her. Adrienne's last wire to Matzhold was on April 26, saying, "We are in seventh heaven."[130]

The honeymoon did not last long. Earle shifted the nature of the relationship. He encouraged Adrienne to perform at the Taksim Kasino, and according to Farago, arranged for her to get a job there.

Matzhold and the Germans were concerned about the change, but maintained hope that the connection was still viable.[131]

From Earle's perspective, and based on defections within German ranks in the months to come, it seems he had decided to treat Adrienne as his own asset in Istanbul and run her against a number of targets. Earle certainly remained in regular contact with Adrienne although now it seems he was employing her to spot and assess various characters and as in informal link for communication. Her association with Earle was well-known. Earle's profile as an old FDR friend; political ally; ambassador to both Austria and Bulgaria; an indiscreet trouble-maker and an unusually effective fixer; and his diplomatically covered posting as "Assistant Naval Attaché" made it all too clear to all the secret services operating in Istanbul that one of the ways to Earle (and perhaps FDR) was via Adrienne. Of course, that route was a two-way street, and Earle was to use it very effectively.

Adrienne quickly established herself at the Taksim Kasino as a nightclub singer and developed a devoted following. An extremely attractive, lithe blonde, with considerable singing and dancing talents, she also enjoyed the image of being connected and in-the-know thanks to Earle. Turkish, German, Soviet and British intelligence services all targeted her to one degree or another. Adrienne seems to have formed a genuine attachment with an Abwehr officer, Dr. Wilhelm Hamburger. "Willy" romanced Adrienne, and they eventually became inseparable.

The relationship between Adrienne and Hamburger is notable because in a two week period late in March 1944, the German intelligence apparatus in Istanbul would suffer three major defections – and they are, in part, attributable to Adrienne and perhaps facilitated or directed by Earle. Quoting the Military Intelligence Service communications intercepts of the Italian Air Attaché from April 5, 1944:

Three sensational flights of officials or agents of the German Secret Services to Allied territory have occurred during the last two weeks. The first to flee was Herr Erich Vermehren, attached to the Information Service of the German Embassy; the second was Herr Karl von Klekowski, of Austrian origin, who disguised what he was doing by calling himself a correspondent of the "Volkischer Beobachter;" the third was Herr Wilhelm Hamburger, a former Austrian, who passed as a merchant.

With regard to Vermehren, the Germans hastened to state that he had absconded with a considerable sum of money. The General Administration of the Turkish Press has forbidden the Turkish newspapers to publish the news that Vermehren's wife is related to Ambassador von Papen. As for Klekowski and Hamburger, it is stated that the German Counterespionage Service has learned that they were engaged in somewhat unorthodox activities with respect to Nazism, and had made arrangements to send them back to Germany.[132]

As time passed, the defections would continue. Late in 1944, Louis Matzhold arrived in Istanbul, looking to reconnect with Adrienne. The two met for dinner at Tokatlyan's and Matzhold wasted no time making the connection to Earle. "How is Hefty?" Matzhold asked, and when Adrienne assured him that Hefty was fine, he came out with the question he had come to Turkey to pop. "Do you think you could arrange a secret meeting with him for me?" he asked. "I would like to make my arrangement with the Americans."[133]

Chapter 9

Canaris and von Papen Approach Earle

We are fortunate to have George Earle's own words describing the clandestine contact by *Abwehr* Chief, Admiral Wilhelm Canaris and German Ambassador to Turkey, Fritz von Papen (via Baron Kurt von Lersner), aimed at neutralizing Hitler and keeping the Soviet Red Army out of Europe. Earle was interviewed in his Radnor, Pennsylvania home in late 1959 by columnist George Fowler. Earle, with Fowler's assistance, published "Roosevelt's Fatal Error," in the March 24, 1960 edition of the magazine *Human Events*:

> Both Canaris and Von Papen were men of no small importance during Nazi Germany's heyday, yet neither man felt any love for Adolph Hitler or his national socialism. They told me that there were men in positions of power in Germany who had formed a network of assassination - a secret grouping of men from military, church, academic, and business circles who saw the destructive path down which Hitler was leading their nation. Their plan was twofold - to kill Hitler and end his mad reign while keeping the Red Army out of Central Europe. They had drafted a constitution for a provisional government to go into effect should the allies approve.
>
> The two, along with Baron Kurt von Lersner. who was in Turkey heading the Orient Society, a German cultural organization, wished me to contact President Roosevelt and outline their plan. Although the Normandy invasion was more than a year away, they were convinced of the

futility of the war, feeling only Russia could come out a
winner if the present trend were not reversed.

It is important at this point to examine the key German
figures making the anti-Hitler approach to Earle. Equally important
is an understanding of how FDR, his administration, the State
Department and OSS comprehended and treated the anti-Nazi
resistance movement in Germany (as opposed to other resistance
movements). It is the critical piece to understanding how events in
Istanbul unfolded and the long-term consequences for US war aims
and "winning the peace."

Before discussing the German resistance operatives who
approached Earle, let us understand why the overture was doomed
to fail. Here is the key to understanding the difference in treatment
of resistance movements: the German anti-Nazi movement was also
anti-Soviet. The strong anti-Soviet objectives of the resistance
movement inside Germany made them unacceptable to FDR. Anti-
Nazis who were anti-Communists were simply not going to be
supported by FDR.

We are indebted to the work and memory of M. Stanton
Evans (*"Stalin's Secret Agents: The Subversion of Roosevelt's
Government"*) for his nearly exhaustive treatment detailing the
Soviet Communists' penetration of the FDR's administration. Evans
names and backs it all up with scrupulous research. We now know
the agents, fellow travelers, cooperators, sympathizers and dupes:
Alger Hiss; Harry Dexter White; Harry Hopkins; Henry Wallace;
Lauchlin Currie; Owen Lattimore; David Niles; and Henry
Morgenthau, among many others – known and still unknown.

Likewise, we have the thoughtful, penetrating analysis of
Diana West (*"American Betrayal: The Secret Assault on Our
Nation's Character"*) that ties the strands of what she calls the "Lost
Narrative" of history together in a way that fills in many historical
blanks and gaps, whether deliberately air-brushed from the

homogenized "Court histories," or simply overlooked. Her treatment of Earle, FDR, this peace initiative and the Katyn Forest Massacre are essential reading.

The anti-Hitler German resistance sought an armistice with the Western Allied powers with the clear, stated objective of stopping the Soviet encroachment into Eastern and Central Europe. OSS Berne Station Chief Allen Dulles stated it clearly in an April 1944 cable:

> The principal motive for their action is the ardent desire to prevent Central Europe from coming ideologically and factually under the control of Russia. They are convinced that in such an event Christian culture and democracy and all that goes with it would disappear in Europe and that the present dictatorship of the Nazis would be exchanged for a new dictatorship.[134]

FDR was not interested. Not in February 1943 and not later. The alliance with "Uncle Joe" Stalin was simply more important.

Admiral Wilhelm Canaris [135]   Franz von Papen[136]

Now to the German officials making overtures to Earle: Canaris, von Papen and von Lersner.

Ladislas Farago had lunch with Admiral (then still Capitan) Wilhelm Canaris in January 1935, shortly after Canaris had taken over the *Abwehr*. Neither man seemed much impressed with the other at the time. Nonetheless, Canaris would go on to revolutionize German military intelligence collection and play a pivotal role in the clandestine dimensions of World War II. Farago, a Hungarian-born journalist covering pre-war Europe would also serve in the intelligence world, then go on to write seminal histories on the subject. Farago's 1967 discovery of a treasure trove of *Abwehr* documents in storage trunks at the National Archives in Washington, DC served as primary source material for much of his work. Farago's sketch of Canaris's career, having obtained 28 of the officer's fitness reports (remarkably intact in post-war Berlin), reveals a consistent trait in the man that biographer Ian Colvin would title, "Master Spy."[137]

Canaris was an extraordinarily resourceful, nearly anonymous, subversive plotter. The Canaris file is impressive: His 1914 escape from a Chilean internment camp (riding cross-country on horseback through Argentina over the Andes) when his ship, *Dresden,* was scuttled following the Battle of the Falkland Islands; slipping undercover through Europe as "Reed Rosas" to rejoin the Navy in order to take command of a submarine; and, his secret role in facilitating the illegal rearmament of the German Navy during the 1920s. Farago sums it up this way: "...Canaris remained the permanent fixture in the conspiratorial consortium, centered in the arch-conservative Navy – the idea man, chief wire-puller, workhorse and troubleshooter, trustee of the Admiral's clique."

Canaris was an efficient staff officer and very comfortable in command – but he had an extra quality. He was a savvy, instinctive intelligence operative. He knew how to get intelligence work done in the field. Not merely an administrator or strategist, he had functioned overseas as an intelligence officer, personally. Farago reports that when Canaris was captured by the Italians in February 1916, attempting to cross the border into Switzerland under his improvised "Reed Rosas" cover he was imprisoned as a suspected spy in a Genoese jail. To escape, Canaris killed an Italian priest, who served as the prison chaplain, stole his habit and fled before being discovered.[138]

The revolutionary advancements in German military intelligence instituted by Canaris are well documented in the works of Ian Colvin and biographer Heinz Höhne. Höhne's treatment runs more than 600 pages and is scrupulously researched and referenced. Höhne introduces us to the means by which Canaris formulated his approach to Earle.

Canaris was driven to action by FDR's pronouncement at the Casablanca Conference:

> ...the Casablanca Conference and the demand for Germany's unconditional surrender spurred Canaris into renewed activity. Now that total disaster threatened the very existence of a country for which generations had fought and striven – for which millions had sacrificed their lives on the battlefields of Europe – Wilhelm Canaris felt a compulsion to act. For one brief moment all his uncertainties and anxieties evaporated. Devious no longer, he set out to conduct a dialogue with the Western Allies by direct means.[139]

Canaris turned to Captain Paul Leverkuehn of the *Abwehr* station in Istanbul. Leverkuehn was an attorney who had worked in New York and Washington DC, and along the way befriended Bill Donovan (later of OSS fame), while Donovan was a Wall Street attorney. Leverkuehn performed legal work for a board chartered to process legal claims arising from World War I. Eventually drafted into the *Wehrmacht*, Leverkuehn worked his way into an intelligence officer position.

Knowing Earle's placement and access to FDR, Leverkuehn proposed Earle to Canaris. He hoped that shared personal experiences between Canaris and Earle, as naval officers and committed anti-Communists would facilitate understanding. To carry forward the fruits of any successful conspiracy between Canaris and Earle, Leverkuehn also settled on the idea of using Ambassador von Papen's own unofficial representative, Baron Kurt von Lersner, to "manage" the contact with Earle.[140] The Canaris-Earle meeting seems to have been set in motion by Captain Leverkuehn.[141]

Importantly, Leverkuehn disassociated himself from the entire affair in his 1954 book, "*German Military Intelligence.*" He reverses the overture, saying it initiated with Earle and that he was "no longer in a position to deal with the matter," and that the task was undertaken by Lersner. Leverkuehn also categorically denies that Canaris made overtures or contacts with the Western Allies, writing: "Nor have I any reason to believe that Canaris at any time sought or made contact with Germany's enemies, though frequent opportunities for such activities were presented to him."[142]

It is difficult to resolve these glaring contradictions illuminated by Leverkuehn. However, given the weight of evidence from multiple other sources (Dulles in Berne, for example) it seems that Leverkuehn was less than forthcoming in his book, or perhaps desired to selectively whitewash parts of the story.

Lauran Paine, in his 1984 history of the *Abwehr*, "German Military Intelligence in World War II," offers another perspective on Leverkuehn, "There were a few blind-loyal followers of Canaris, such as Dr. Leverkuehn who refused to believe this [anti-Hitler motives of Canaris], and it does not help that those in Britain's intelligence organizations with full knowledge of these matters have maintained an obdurate silence."[143] Perhaps it was blind loyalty.

Baron von Lersner's involvement brings us to the German ambassador to Turkey: Franz Joseph Hermann Michael Maria von Papen, *Erbsälzer zu Werl und Neuwerk* (a hereditary aristocratic title from the region of Werl in North Rhine–Westphalia).

Franz von Papen was a conservative, Catholic aristocrat and the last Chancellor before Hitler. He served as an officer in the Imperial German Army and was selected for training as a General Staff officer. He served as military attaché to the United States from 1913 to 1915, and traveled to Mexico organizing elements of the Mexican Revolution and planning acts of sabotage against the United States. He was expelled from the United States in 1915 and went on to command an infantry battalion in First World War. When the war ended, he was a lieutenant colonel serving in the Middle East theatre.

Von Papen led a *Freikorps* unit in the Ruhr against Communist uprising in 1920 and became a leader of the largely Catholic *Zentrum* political party. By 1932, President Paul von Hindenburg appointed von Papen Chancellor. He came to believe that Hitler could be controlled by conservative political forces and the General Staff, suggesting to Hindenburg that Hitler replace him as Chancellor, while von Papen serve as Hitler's Vice-Chancellor.

Aggressive consolidation of power by Hitler and the Nazi Party forced von Papen from office, whereupon he accepted appointments as Ambassador to Vienna ('34 to '38, and briefly overlapping with Earle), and then Ankara ('39 to '44).

In his "*Memoirs*" (1953), von Papen identifies his overtures to Earle with the efforts of what became known as the *Kreisau* Circle – the German resistance cell headed by Helmuth James von Moltke (working as a lawyer under Canaris in the *Abwehr*), and represented

in the person of Dr. Adam von Trott zu Solz, a member of the
German Foreign Ministry holding the rank of Legation Secretary.[144]

Trott was a personal friend and legal colleague of
Leverkuehn, dating back to the mid-1930s. This personal and
professional relationship seems certain to have facilitated Trott's
regular travel to Turkey on official business and been particularly
helpful during the early 1943 visit when he endeavored to make a
compelling argument to von Papen. Trott is a fascinating character
in his own right, and Christopher Sykes's book, *"Tormented
Loyalty"* (1969) paints a compelling portrait of a German aristocrat
who paid the price of his life in August 1944 for defying Hitler.[145]

Interestingly, the *Kreisau* Circle had its doubts about von
Papen. Klemens von Klemperer, in his *"German Resistance Against
Hitler: The Search for Allies Abroad, 1938 – 1945,"* discusses
Trott's mission to von Papen:

> There his [Trott's] chief objective was to persuade … von
> Papen … to join the conspiracy. Papen had weathered
> many a storm during the Nazi regime, whether by virtue
> of his agility or his fickleness. But while official Nazi
> Germany still considered him something of an asset, in
> particular as a window to the outside world, the
> Resistance thought of him as a pivotal person of potential
> value to it. No one harboured any illusions about Papen.
> He was known to be weak and vacillating … he was
> thought of in opposition circles as a possible ally.[146]

Trott gained von Papen's assistance, but was not able to
bring the Ambassador around to full, explicit allegiance with the
Kreisau Circle. Ambassador von Papen delegated the contact effort
with Earle, and all subsequent meetings with the FDR's emissary to
Baron von Lersner.[147] As we have discussed, this all seems to have
been synchronized through the efforts of *Abwehr*-Istanbul Chief,
Leverkuehn.

Baron von Lersner had a long and distinguished diplomatic career, while having the unenviable and domestically ignoble position of heading the German delegation to the Paris Peace Conference. His presidency of the "German Orient Society" in Istanbul served two purposes. It kept the Baron safe from Nazi ethnic purity scrutiny (as he was believed to have a Jewish ancestor) and allowed him to serve as an unofficial channel of communication for von Papen.

Von Lersner made contact with Earle and the two men had a series of intermittent meetings that spanned more than a year.

Returning to Earle's published record from March 1960 in *Human Events*:

> Although I was aware of the menace of Russian expansion and felt that the plan had great possibilities. I knew little more than most people in the allied camp about the extent of the anti-Nazi movement in Germany. Among those who sought to overthrow the dictator long before the war began to go against Germany were General Ludwig Von Beck, onetime head of the German General Staff, Herbert Bismarck, State Secretary of the Prussian Ministry and grandson of the "Iron Chancellor," and Heinrich Brüning, former Chancellor and the leading Catholic intellectual in Germany.

> My first contact with the anti-Hitlerites came a few days after I checked into my Istanbul hotel. While in my room one morning, I was visited by a short, middle-aged man in civilian clothes, who identified himself as Admiral Wilhelm Canaris. Canaris told me he was disturbed by the Allied policy of unconditional surrender, and that it meant nothing but good for the Russians and ill for the Western nations. He exclaimed that those in Germany who felt they could get rid of Hitler if they could deal with the Americans had very little bargaining power left. "This means war to the end, the destruction of Germany as a military power, and the emergence of Russia as the dominating force in Europe," Canaris said.

Earle just described one of the most audacious and astounding clandestine acts of the Second World War. It is also probably the least known German resistance overtures and one of the best kept secrets of the entire era. The very notion of the Chief of German Military Intelligence making a direct approach to the personal emissary of the President of the United States to sue for an armistice and offer Hitler in return is astounding.

One wonders why that piece of history was suppressed. Certainly more people have some level of awareness of the May 1941 solo flight of Deputy Fuhrer Rudolph Hess to Scotland in a curious, failed, peace bid than any knowledge of the Canaris/Earle meeting. The irony is that the Canaris/Earle meeting actually had some possibility for real success, had FDR had any legitimate interest in ending the war. Perhaps that is it? The "court history" and victor's propaganda simply does not allow for inconvenient, factual narratives to take hold or gain purchase in the contemporary conscience of establishment history. Legacy preservation trumps reality. Perhaps it is because of the "messenger" – Earle, himself – not the OSS, the State Department, or some other government entity with a public affairs office? Nonetheless, we have Earle's firsthand account that we now return to …

> I agreed with Canaris that Roosevelt's policy contained disastrous implications, and, sensing something important, I asked what he had in mind. He asked me whether I thought Roosevelt actually meant "unconditional" surrender. "Our generals will never swallow such a policy," Canaris said. "What terms would they consider?" I asked.

Here the controversy swirls, once again, over FDR's Casablanca Conference announcement concerning "unconditional surrender." Perhaps FDR truly considered it a PR stunt or jingoistic rhetoric that was "suitable" for press purposes, but not the literal policy position of the Allies. The British claimed to have been surprised by the use of the term. Likewise FDR's civilian and military staff, but the language quickly cemented itself in the publics' conscience. The reception of the language and its full meaning was clearly something the Germans had not fully worked out. Earle continues, quoting Canaris ...

> Perhaps you will take the matter up with your President, the German suggested. I am leaving Istanbul this afternoon. I will return in 60 days. I hope you will have something to tell me.

> Canaris had indeed been vague, but it seemed a valid feeler and I wrote the President, detail. My dispatch went off by plane in the next diplomatic pouch. Impatiently I waited, but no reply came.

Earle would reveal in subsequent Congressional testimony (in 1947 and 1952) that silence was a routine FDR tactic – part of the President's standing operating procedure for situations and circumstances when things were in conflict or at odds with his ideas, priorities or policies. Rather than overtly and explicitly disagree or argue over contested issues, FDR would simply "go quiet." FDR did not want to document disagreement or bring things to a head in an open way. Subordinates would simply not hear back or get a definitive decision. Such was this case with Earle.

> Two months later my phone rang and I recognized the voice of Admiral Canaris. "I'm the gentleman who called on you unannounced two months ago. Has there been any progress in the matter we discussed?"

> I thought of my urgent unanswered message to Roosevelt, then answered: "No, no progress."

> "I am very sorry," Canaris said, and hung up.

This moment is pivotal for the German *Widerstand*, because they viewed it as a foreclosure on a negotiated Allied armistice with a hope towards turning in a united front against the greatest threat to

Western Civilization – the Bolsheviks of the Soviet Union. FDR's non-response changed everything. The *Widerstand* were truly on their own. Elsewhere around the globe, Allied governments and forces had assisted resistance movements against the Axis powers and the occupations – but not for Germany. The people that could actually kill or deliver Hitler would not be supported or cooperated with in any way. There is a bitter irony here, of course, when one considers the enormous loss of life and destruction of property that 18 additional months of war cost Europe. That bitterness turns to ashes when one then considers how all of Eastern Europe was then surrendered to the Soviets for decades of repression and domination. Despite this staggering disappointment, the channel between Earle and the *Widerstand* remained open and planning continued. Contingencies and unforeseen developments made it prudent to make the most of the presidential emissary's time and effort. Earle goes on to explain …

> Although I was unhappy about the Canaris incident. I began to hear whispers along the Istanbul diplomatic grape vine that Baroness Von Papen, wife of the German ambassador, was uttering strong anti-Hitler and anti-Nazi remarks in private conversations. She was reported to have called the top Nazis "besotted men, ridden with savage inferiority complexes." The Von Papens were very close, and Franz was a devout Catholic - hardly a man to embrace Hitler's philosophy.
>
> My next contact with the Germans was not with the Von Papens, but with Kurt Von Lersner, the cultural group head. He had led the German delegation during the Versailles Peace Conference after the First World War and was now in comparative exile because of a fraction of Jewish blood. Von Lersner called me at my hotel. Although I had met him previously we hadn't talked politics. This time he said. "I have read about you in our Nazi press. Also. I am acquainted with some of your views on Russia. We have many things in common." Von

Lersner pointed out my direct connection with the President went back to the early thirties, when I was Governor of Pennsylvania - the first Democrat to hold that job in 44 years.

Detecting key innuendoes in his conversation, I realized we had much to say to each other, but not over the phone. We decided to meet at nine that night, each driving alone to an appointed spot about five miles out of Istanbul.

Earle would eventually have a number of clandestine meetings with Lersner (and others that are hinted at, but never identified) to discuss the details of what Earle's role might be in a liaison capacity between the German and Allied armies. Earle's description of the *Widerstand's* goals and the meeting details continues ...

The meeting lasted more than three hours, during which we discussed many matters pertaining to the war. Von Lersner was much less cryptic than Canaris had been. He told me that many high placed officials in Germany, Von Papen included, loved the Fatherland and hated the Fuhrer, feeling that he was leading their nation to destruction. He said they wanted to end the war before Hitler bled Germany of all its youth resources. They were concerned with the menace of the Soviet Union, an enemy they understood and knew must be stopped.

At that nocturnal meeting Von Lersner posed the following question: If the anti-Nazi forces delivered the German Army to the Allies, could they count on Allied cooperation in keeping the Russian Army out of Germany and Central Europe? If Roosevelt would interest himself in their plan, he said, they would go ahead with their risky idea to assassinate Hitler and arrange for an honorable surrender preparatory to the formation of a democratic government. Von Lersner assured me that, even if Hitler were not killed, the latter would be turned over to the Allies as a war criminal.

Writing 15 years after the war, Earle's narrative is about to take a critical turn against the Communists and the frustration he felt against key figures in the FDR White House …

> Again I made coded contact with the White House. pleading with Roosevelt to pursue what these anti-Nazis had to offer. As the weeks passed the Red Army continued to grind its way westward, feeding itself on the tools of war Roosevelt's lend lease program provided. I continually pressed the matter with hopeless communiques, until at last I sensed the real snag: Von Lersner and his anti-Nazi countrymen had taken an absolute stand against Communist expansion, and this was disturbing to FDR – a man who had great faith in the integrity of his friend Joe Stalin. During the late spring and early summer months of 1943, Von Lersner kept after me - but still no word of encouragement was received from Washington.
>
> During the summer of '43 Von Lersner called with a new note of elation in his voice. "Now you'll see. We have something definite to offer." We agreed to meet that night.

To students of the *Widerstand*, the details of Lersner's plan for the seizure of Hitler by the Boeslager Cavalry unit at Hitler's Prussian headquarters lends an enormous amount of credibility to the information Earle was able to glean – and important insights into the military planning of the resistance leadership. Earle's detailed reporting continues …

> Von Lersner wasted no time in outlining the fantastic yet practical plan his cohorts were ready to hatch against Hitler. Aside from top Germans already mentioned, the plotters included Count Wolf Heinrich Von Helldorf, chief of police of Berlin, Freiherr Von Boeslager, a well-known German cavalry officer, and others of importance.
>
> Boeslager and his cavalry brigade were ready to surround Hitler's remote Wolfchanze (Wolf's Lair), the Fuhrer's East Prussian forest headquarters. The cavalrymen were

to move in on signal and capture both Hitler and Gestapo chief Heinrich Himmler. Top Nazis would be imprisoned and held for Allied trials. Beck and other Junker officers in the plot would assume military command and move all German troops to the Eastern front until a cease fire could be arranged.

This development in the dialogue between Earle and von Lersner – and the level of specificity in the German plan, as well as its explicit communication to Earle, is an extraordinary development and revelation far beyond other "peace feeler" anecdotes from across Europe – whether they came through the OSS, State Department or allied intelligence sources. Earle was prepared to fly to an airfield north of Berlin to facilitate the communication of the guarantee to the German Resistance and to act as the Allied liaison for the coup against Hitler.[148]

Von Lersner was referring to *Reiterabteilung* (cavalry detachment) Boeselager, an extraordinary, elite armored unit formed in January 1943 under the command of Georg Freiherr von Boeselager, consisting of two battalions each of five squadrons of 220 men. The unit also was referred to as "Cavalry Regiment Center," and was designed to operate independently, rather than as smaller detachments assigned to scout and screen for infantry divisions. A substantial number of the soldiers were reportedly Russian Cossacks. The anti-Hitler conspirators now had a reliable elite force whose officers were at least sympathetic, if not committed to the resistance.[149]

Returning to Earle's narrative:

Before Von Lersner and I parted, I expressed my sympathy for the right thinking and courageous people of Germany - who were faced with the behemoth task of throwing off the Nazi yoke while repulsing the ogre of Red Russian expansion. I promised to do my best with Roosevelt, and we parted in solemn accord.

Within a few hours my new dispatches to Roosevelt were on their way. To be sure that the all-important messages got through, I sent them by Army and Navy channels as well as the regular State Department diplomatic pouch. Although I was excited and optimistic as I sent them on their way, I should have known better. The President was under the spell of the Soviet leader and the wartime White House was no place to tell the truth about Russia. Strong influences who had the President's ear wanted to see Germany wiped out, regardless of the cost in American lives.

Writing in 1960, with the hindsight of lost opportunities and the extreme tensions of the Cold War mounting, it is easy to appreciate Earle's frustrations for a resolution to what might have been. It is clearly very difficult to have been at the very edge of an opportunity for a very different future and then see it slip away. The consequences were both profound and unnecessary. That seems to have haunted Earle for the rest of his life.

All the Germans required was Roosevelt's signature on a document stating the single condition that my contacts had relayed to me. If the President sent back a positive answer, I was to arrange to meet a plane which was to land outside Istanbul and fly me to Germany to set terms with Hitler's enemies. Everything was set for the flight, but as the days passed I grew increasingly discouraged. Finally I received an answer from President Roosevelt: "All such applications for a negotiated peace should be referred to the Supreme Allied Commander, General Eisenhower."

Although phrased in diplomatic terms, this was an absolute brushoff - the type of answer scores of associates learned to expect from FDR. Here was a clear-cut indication that the President had no interest in a valid plan laid by desperate but honest men to end the war and save countless lives.

The approach to Earle and detailed descriptions of the anti-Hitler resistance plans and preparedness to act did not occur in a vacuum. Other tracks and initiatives from the Kreisau Circle occurred concurrently in Switzerland, Sweden and Spain.

In their biography, *"Helmuth von Moltke: A Leader Against Hitler,"* Malcolm Balfour and Julian Frisby describe von Moltke's travel to Istanbul, contacts with the OSS, and efforts to meet with Alexander Kirk, the US Ambassador in Cairo. The official, Canaris-approved, cover for von Moltke's trip to Turkey (5-10 July 1943) was to settle a legal question with the Turkish government over the return to Germany of a fleet of French-owned Danubian ships interned in the Sea of Marmara.[150]

Balfour and Frisby include both a letter from von Moltke to Kirk and a lengthy resistance policy document detailing *Widerstand* willingness to cooperate with the Western Allies that was reportedly conveyed via OSS channels to FDR. The policy document had the unwieldy title: "Exposé on the Readiness of a Powerful German Group to Prepare and Assist Allied Military Operations Against Nazi Germany."[151] Both the letter and the policy document were viewed with deep suspicion.[152]

Canaris biographer Höhne views the von Moltke trip to Istanbul and the production of documents as a sequel or next phase of the approach to Earle. Von Lersner had discussed the possibility of Earle flying to Germany and serving as the Allied liaison contact for an armistice link-up between the warring armies. The man at the appointed time and place that would transition the war on the Western Front to a peace that could then be leveraged against the real threat to Christendom and civilization: The Soviet Army. Von Moltke's approach now discussed a variation on that theme, with a German Staff Officer of sufficient rank and knowledge to serve as the liaison to the Allies.[153]

In addition to von Moltke's letter to Kirk and the resistance policy document, a third document (from 1944) comes into the mix. *Abwehr*-Istanbul chief Paul Leverkuehn apparently wrote a letter on

German embassy letterhead that was brought to the US by OSS chief Donovan and subsequently analyzed by Stanford University professor Karl Brandt who concluded it was genuine. Nonetheless, FDR rejected engaging with "these East German *Junkers*."[154]

Balfour and Frisby accept American confusion and suspicion over the multiple resistance overtures.[155] One might argue in the alternative that rather than confusion and suspicion, the multiple and compounding efforts of the *Widerstand* were the desperate measures of people gripped by genuine desperation. That the multi-pronged approach was a near-last ditch effort to both thwart Nazi domestic countersubversion efforts and find some open channel to communicate effectively with senior American leaders and FDR.

Earle continued his March 1960 remembrance, describing his White House meeting with FDR:

> In May, 1944, I flew to Washington to see the President. While waiting in an ante-room in the White House, I met Secretary of the Navy James Forrestal. This was five years before his tragic suicide. I conveyed my fears of Russia, and within the shadow of the President's desk Forrestal told me: "My God, George, you and I and Bill Bullitt are the only ones around the President who know the Russian leaders for what they really are."

> When I went in to see the President he was his usual self, full of humor, his ego riding high. "Mr. President," I said, "the real menace is not Germany, it is Russia." FDR gave me a patronizing smile and said: "George, Russia is a nation of 180 million people speaking 120 different dialects. When the war is over she will fly to pieces like a cracked centrifugal machine at high speed."

> In Germany the anti-Nazis realized they would get no help from FDR and decided to go ahead with their plan to kill Hitler. America's disinterest undoubtedly caused many plotters to back out and brought serious gaps in the plan.[156]

FDR's categorical rejection of the Earle-Canaris-von Papen channel, as well as the other resistance overtures, prolonged World War II. The last resort of the resistance came to be the July 20, 1944 bomb plot executed by Colonel Claus Graf von Stauffenberg at Hitler's *Wolfsschanze* (Wolf's Lair) headquarters in East Prussia.

In February 1944, a year after the German resistance overtures and a few months before Earle's May 1944 meeting with FDR, something in the White House posture towards Earle changed dramatically. Newly uncovered records from the National Archives (specifically FDR's White House Naval Aides File) show a file marked: "TOP SECRET DATA RE EARLE CASE." The file contains intercepted diplomatic cables from Greek, Japanese, Nationalist Chinese and Spanish officials discussing Earle's activities in Istanbul from January 1944 to December 1944. The subjects range from the Soviet Army's westward advance into Europe, to Earle's intrigues in the Balkans, to various German peace initiatives.[157]

What is remarkable, of course, is that the FDR White House had a Top Secret case open on Earle – and that the most sophisticated intelligence gathering techniques of the WWII era – communications intelligence intercept – were being used to target a personal emissary of the President. Did FDR order the opening of a case file on Earle? Did Harry Hopkins or some other senior White House official? What was the motive for opening such a file? What was the "Earle Case?"

Chapter 10

Earle's Reporting to FDR from Istanbul

While the German overtures to Earle were remarkable, if not stunning developments – particularly the personal meeting with Admiral Canaris – they were hardly the only intelligence developments and intrigues unfolding in Istanbul. Foreign diplomatic and intelligence officers – Axis and Allied – were keenly interested in Earle's activities and contacts. British journalist Cedric Salter of *The Daily Mail*, warned Earle that an MI6 operative, Colonel Thompson, "a former CID Inspector and head of the 'killing' branch of British Intelligence in the Middle East," was determined to discredit Earle because he was, "the next worse enemy of the British."[158]

Earle's son, Lawrence (himself an OSS officer in the Pacific theatre of operations), described in personal interviews with the author multiple efforts of unknown assailants to assassinate his father by forcing him off the road and over cliffs along dangerous roads in rural Turkey.[159]

Earle had an established network of diplomatic, governmental, business, and social contacts throughout the Balkans and reaching into Central Europe. That fact is easily understood given his extensive personal travels throughout Europe before the war, as well as his ambassadorial postings to Vienna and Sofia. It is also easy to comprehend given his gregarious personal nature, generosity, keen intellect and sense of adventure. He worked his contacts, developed and exploited relationships and sought new opportunities in the unique environment Istanbul presented. The assistant air attaché at the German embassy, an Austrian with strong anti-Nazi sentiments, became a valuable source.[160]

Earle may have been the very first Allied intelligence officer to verify the earlier reporting of the savagery the Russians had inflicted on the Poles in the Katyn Forest. His sources in Central Europe were telling him in graphic detail what was rumored in Western Europe – that it was the Soviets who responsible for the 1940 slaughter. The news was unwelcome to FDR, who would encourage Earle to investigate further – the results of which would later become a breaking point between the two men.

Earle provided reporting on the Ploesti oil field raids in Romania. He also provided critical predictive information on both German V-1 "buzz bomb" and V-2 rocket attacks on the UK, that were corroborated and later confirmed to FDR by Churchill in cables between the two leaders. More alarming to FDR was Earle's report that a, "Stratospheric attack on America will follow." Earle warned of the targeting of the US East Coast with a "V-3" rocket. Reconnaissance photographs of German submarines outfitted with launch ramps affixed to their decks, as well as towed launch platforms fueled concerns over the Germans' ability to move rockets via submarine off the US coast and then attack New York and Washington. While those attacks never came, it did not mean the Germans were not preparing and testing with that objective in mind. The reporting seemed to corroborate "Magic" communications intelligence decrypts of Japanese diplomatic transmissions describing further German successes in the development, production and fielding of the Me-264 long-range strategic bomber.[161]

Earle sent a cable to Harry Hopkins on September 13, 1943 with a strongly worded assessment of the state of affairs in Central Europe and the Balkans – it is classic George Earle reporting and analysis:

The three newly appointed Bulgarian Regents are completely controlled by Nazis. The new Premier Gabrovsky is the most extreme Nazi in Bulgaria – a cold blooded sadistic torturer and killer. In order to bring the Bulgarian people to a realization of their true position and what suffering lies in store for them if they do not oust their present government and the Germans, I strongly advocate the following course of action. First, with radio and leaflets to give them fifteen to thirty days warning of the punishment to be meted out to them if they do not repudiate by some means their present government and the German alliance. Second, if results are not apparent within allotted time, to bomb railway yards at Sofia. The Bulgarians treasure Sofia as the Hungarians do Budapest and after the destruction of railway yards, I would give them fifteen days to reflect before completely smashing Sofia and other cities. I feel certain this course of action would not only be beneficial for our portion of Bulgaria, but would make a powerful impression on Rumania and be most heartening and stimulating for the Yugoslav and Greek patriots.[162]

Earle sent FDR a letter dated October 1, 1943 wherein he recaps the importance of the upcoming election and FDR's inevitable victory. He goes on to provide the President with a key, and soon to be recurring, insight:

The most important and most difficult problem you will have to face in post war Europe will be Russia. This country, today probably the most popular in America and England , thirty days after the cessation of hostilities will be the most unpopular, due not to Bolshevism but to Russian imperialism.[163]

On March 24, 1944, Earle wrote a cover letter to FDR and attached an 11-page, single-spaced, typed report from a German source, and transmitted it to the president via diplomatic pouch. The report is a sweeping political analysis of Soviet Communist objectives in Europe, with a country-by-country analysis. The Earle cover letter, however, has tremendous value in understanding the growing rift between the presidential emissary and the FDR White House. Written on the letterhead of the Office of the Naval Attaché, Earle conveyed the following:

> Istanbul, 24 March 1944
>
> My dear Mr. President:
>
> The enclosed was handed to me by a member of the Gestapo, who says (falsely, I think) that he wants to come over to us. It is undoubtedly German propaganda, the only good propaganda Germany has.
>
> However, propaganda to be effective must be at least 80% true.
>
> It is this element of truth that worries me.
>
> Is America giving its life blood to exchange one bunch of gangsters for another as masters of Europe, and as a world menace?
>
> Mr. President, <u>please</u> read this. You are in so much a better position to analyze it than I.
>
> I have one great regret, and that is your critics in America do not know the tremendous, overwhelming popularity you have in the Near East.
>
> Cordially and respectfully yours,
>
> /s/
>
> George H. Earle.
>
> The President,
> The White House

The FDR library file copy of the Earle letter contains a vertical, handwritten, mark next to the "gangster" paragraph. We know that FDR read the report. A memo from the President to Admiral Leahy on May 24, 1944 states: "Will you read the enclosed and let me know what you think I should do about it?" Two days later, Leahy responds to FDR: "There is of course and element of truth in this German propaganda. Even if it were 100% true and 100% objectionable to America there appears to be nothing we can do about it until Hitler is defeated. I suggest sending Lieutenant Commander Earle's letter with its enclosures to the Department of State for its information." [164]

Earle sent a classified, encrypted, Naval message to FDR on April 13, 1944 with message handling instructions: "REQUESTED DELIVERY TO THE PRESIDENT BY LT COMDR EARLE." The message read:

> I believe Russian menace today greater than Nazi ever was for the following reasons:
>
> 1.   Although Bolshevists and Nazis are both reigns of terror from many refuges I learn excepting treatment of Jews Bolshevists are the more barbarous in treatment of occupied territories liquidating cruelly all those with any education or wealth.
>
> 2.   If Germany capitulates occupation or conquest of Europe by Russia far easier than for Nazis because all Europe is either actively or passively against Nazis whereas 60% of Europeans today because of losses and suffering are communistically inclined. There exists today large communist party in Germany. If Russia occupies Germany and Bolshevizes it what force on Earth can stop a combination of Russian and German manpower and German industrial ability.
>
> 3.   Stalin's promises have been proved worthless by Russian action in Baltic states and encouragement to Poland with promises of Russian aid should she enter war against Germany.
>
> 4.   Russian wants to see Japan and Anglo/Saxon nations bleed each other to death. In my opinion neutrality is the best we can hope for from Russia in our war with Japan. [165]

Four days later, on April 17, 1944, Earle sent another seemingly prescient cable directly to FDR, classified "Secret," with the handling instructions, "COMDR EARLE REQUESTS DELIVERY TO PRESIDENT ROOSEVELT." Earle wrote:

> With Germany's capitulation not far off the menace of Russia to world peace and security grows more threatening daily. The civilization that controls the Arabian oil will probably play the dominant role in future. Turkey believes in Anglo Saxon civilization and is ready to support it against Russian brand. Turkey is a logical geographical and political barrier to future Russian aggression in the Middle East. Advise strengthening her instead of weakening her in the Anglo Americans expect to control Arabian oil and play a leading part in the world of tomorrow.[166]

The FDR archive note for this message from Earle notes that on May 2, 1944, "Admiral Leahy says no further action will be taken at this time."

On July 8, 1944 Earle sent a handwritten letter to Admiral Wilson Brown in his clean, rounded, rolling penmanship. He wrote:

> When I was ordered to this post in January 1943, it was understood that I was to report directly to the President. In order, however, to save the President as much as possible was to send my reports through Harry Hopkins so he could screen out a lot of what I would send in that might be duplication or not important enough.
>
> Harry's health is not too good and as he is away from the White House a great deal, Captain Heard [Deputy Director of Naval Intelligence] was kind enough to suggest I send my reports to you.
>
> Personally, I see no reason they should not be given in their entirety to the Navy Department if you think there is enough interest.
>
> Very respectfully yours,
> George H. Earle

P.S. I regret I do not know typewriting & have no one I
can trust to do this for me.
GHE[167]

Earle included a handwritten page and a half "Report to
Naval Aide of President" [Admiral Wilson Brown] with three
points:

> 1.   Representatives of the Polish Government in
> Istanbul are greatly worried by the defection of one of
> their minor officials here, Opaienski by name, who has
> sold out completely to the Germans. The Poles fear the
> Russians here will learn of it and make a serious incident
> out of it for Anti Polish [sic] propaganda.
>
> 2.   Reports from good sources indicate the underground
> campaign of the Communists in Poland with the Polish
> peasants to make them bitter against the great landowners
> in Poland because of the very bad distribution of land in
> Poland, is effective. If successful, it will mean a distinct
> trend in sympathy to Russia and a corresponding
> widening rift between Polish peasants and the Polish
> Government in London.
>
> 3.   From several fair Russian sources I learn Premier
> Stalin is suffering from serious heart disease, probably
> angina pectoris. Although certain well informed Turks
> believe his successor in case of death would be Foreign
> Commissar Molotoff, a good Russian source informs me
> it would be Tcherbakoff, former chief assistant to Berea,
> Chief of the N.K.V.D.. [sic] Tcherbakoff is now Assistant
> to Stalin as Minister of War. My informant says
> Tcherbakoff is about forty two years of age, very
> energetic, rather able, completely in Stalin's confidence,
> and a thorough Terrorist as would be expected from a
> former Assistant Chief of the N.K.V.D..[sic]
>
> George H. Earle

Earle's contacts, information and instincts on conditions in
Poland are important and foreshadow his role in unraveling the

controversy of the Katyn Forest Massacre. His Soviet political intelligence on the heart health of Stalin and the Soviet pecking order in Moscow was sure to have been another tile in the mosaic of Kremlinology. Earle appears to be referencing Alexander Shcherbakov (or variously, Sherbakoff), former secretary of the Moscow Communist Party, director of the "Soviet Information Bureau," and political director of the Red Army, who died an alcoholic death with complications from heart disease in May 1945.

George Earle's good-natured personal temperament and commitment to fostering the individual liberties enshrined in our Bill of Rights shines through in another handwritten note to Admiral Leahy dated July 22, 1944. Earle takes the time to highlight a suggestion made by his nominal superior, Captain Webb Trammell, USN, the Naval Attaché in Ankara. Trammell's goal was the creation of an international panel or conference promoting freedom of the press and the "free exchange of news and other information" in the post-war era. On July 15, 1944, the State Department adopted the idea and Earle wanted to get on the record in the White House assigning credit to Trammell. Earle made sure Admiral Leahy knew he had communicated the same information about Trammell's proposal two months earlier to FDR, Senator Barkley and J. David Stern, the Editor of the *Philadelphia Record*. Earle wanted Trammell appointed to the proposed commission associated with this international, First Amendment-style initiative.[168]

Reporting on Romania was dispatched by Earle to Admiral Leahy on August 16, 1944. Once again, Earle affixed a handwritten cover letter to typed "report" – this time from "the best Romanian source." The Romanian document is largely an apologia for Romanian cooperation with the Germans, with an eye towards the increasingly apparent Allied victory and new order to be imposed on Bucharest.

The most significant information in the report was probably the updated German order of battle report detailing the withdrawal of three German armored divisions, one infantry division and a portion of Luftwaffe assets. The assessed strength of the German Wehrmacht in Romania stood at approximately 15 divisions. The source reported that the Romanian army was in a numerically superior position to both the German occupying forces and that only a "promise of better peace conditions" administered by all of the Allied powers (and not just the Russians) would bring the Romanians "over to our side."[169] The "report" manages to be both an extraordinarily arrogant and naive document in the same stroke. Much of the "political analysis" is self-serving and superficial in accounting for Romania's active cooperation with the Nazis. Likewise, the opportunistic "eye to the future" tone of the peace conditions "acceptable" to the Nazi collaborators is striking.

As fate would have it, Earle's reporting became moot within a few days, as King Michael I of Romania led a successful coup against the Axis powers and the Antonescu dictatorship. Within two weeks, King Michael and his government would be officially part of the Allies with full recognition by all of the major powers.[170] The rapidly developing situation in Central Europe and the Balkans would later be acknowledged by Admiral Wilson Brown to Earle in a September 1 message noting Earle's valuable reporting and the tempo of events.

Despite earlier representations to Harry Hopkins and Admirals Leahy and Brown, seeking their assistance in screening and evaluating his reporting, Earle would exercise is extraordinary authority to communicate directly with the President on August 22, 1944. Earle's typewritten single page embassy letterhead memo conveys a 16-page report authored by Vichy French diplomat Gaston Bergery. Earle wrote to FDR:

Istanbul, August 22, 1944

My dear Mr. President:

The enclosure with this letter I consider the most important communication I have ever sent you. I beg of you to read it very carefully.

It is written by Bergerie [sic] former French Ambassador to Russia, and now Vichy Ambassador to Turkey. He considers you, in his words, "the greatest humanitarian of modern times." He has written it for you alone, not as an Ambassador nor as a French Deputy, nor as an owner of a Paris newspaper but as an individual who admires your courage, resourcefulness and sincerity.

About Russia, I fear he is right.

May I make two observations. An American banker said to me a few weeks ago, "we should have been warned of Japan's intentions by the simple fact that every Japanese tourist in America was pictured with a camera, and American tourists were not permitted cameras in Japan!" In the same way I say by the fact Russia will not permit our soldiers to fight with them nor our correspondents to go to the front should warn us of Russia's intentions.

Also, and far more important is the fact that the moment fighting is over, there will be irresistible pressure from the people of the Democracies to demobilize and return home our soldiers. There will be no such pressure to demobilize the Russian soldiers since the lot of a Russian is far more comfortable in the army than at home.

My most fervent hope is that a year from today you can say, "George Earle was a fool and an alarmist."

Cordially and respectfully yours,

/s/

George H. Earle[171]

The President,
The White House

The 16-page Bergery attachment to Earle's letter is an analysis from the perspective of the Vichy Government of Marshal Philippe Pétain of the post-war "Russia problem." One of the opening lines of the assessment is: "The Russia problem is usually treated with a combined lack of knowledge and serious thought." Interestingly, one of the "classes" of persons described as having particular attitudes and beliefs concerning Russia appears to fit perfectly with the FDR White House and what Earle would encounter with the President over the Katyn Forest Massacre. Specifically, Bergery describes:

> A third class of people have decided to display and extraordinary "agnosticism" and do not want to hear anything about a russia [sic] problem, because it presently disturbs the comfortable line of thought they have been driven into by the radio and the press : viz. that there is a big black wolf called Germany, after the destruction of which the world will be happy and free for ever. These people, when placed before certain uncomfortable facts, just answer "it's all German propaganda."[172]

That response is, literally, what FDR told Earle in the White House in March 1945. Earle's expressed hope – that within a year he would be called a fool and an alarmist – may have been the wishful thinking of FDR and his staff, but was sadly not the historical foundation of post-war Europe and the impending Cold War.

An August 26, 1944 letter from Earle to Admiral Brown contained four "exhibits" of reporting concerning Russia from French, Polish and White Russian sources, plus some reporting on Romania. The reports were broadly anti-communist and speculative – consistently warning of the true intentions of Stalin in a post-war Europe.

Earle received positive feedback from the White House on the reporting and commentary he provided. On September 1, 1944, Brown wrote:

> I am sorry to be so late in acknowledging your various letters, all of which I believe have reached me quite promptly. Events are moving so rapidly that the information is sometimes outdated, as with your latest letter of August 16th, but on the other hand I know that the President is glad to have your opinion of what is going on and what is developing.
>
> I shall, of course, always be glad to pass along whatever you send me.
>
> With all good wishes,
> Sincerely yours,
>
> Wilson Brown
> Rear Admiral, U.S.N.
> Naval Aide to the President

A letter from Earle to Admiral Brown on September 3, 1944 reveals significant animosity by Earle towards the British, and may provide some context for *Daily Mail* journalist Cedric Salter's comments on the interest of Colonel Thompson of MI6 in targeting and discrediting Earle. In describing a White Russian behind the sourcing of some reporting, Earle states, "The British have persuaded the Turks to deport him to Egypt." Earle then continues:

> The British are determined we shall have no influence and little to say in the Balkans and the Near East, except when they do something unpleasant to these peoples when we are taken in as more than equal partners with them.
>
> The Bulgarian agent who was transmitting messages between King Boris and myself was refused a Turkish visa under British pressure, and now this White Russian, again under British pressure, who was giving me valuable information, is deported to Egypt.

It is interesting how history repeats itself. We fought the Revolution in 1776 because of "taxation without representation!" Now 168 years later we are again being taxed hundreds of thousands of lives and billions of dollars to save the British Empire and again they don't want us to have any "representation." However, I guess we've got to get along with them somehow.[173]

Earle's reporting to FDR is not without humor. A handwritten letter dated October 31, 1944, discusses French General Charles de Gaulle:

My dear Mr. President:

Yesterday, Doctor Gassiu, with the French Army rank of Colonel, who is head of the Pasteur Hospital here, said to me in the strictest confidence: "I have had many opportunities of observing General de Gaulle. I will stake my reputation as a medical man that General de Gaulle is a paranoiac with a slow but progressive trend towards delusion and insanity!"

Whether this opinion is an accurate diagnosis or something wholly untrue given me with the intention of prejudicing me against General de Gaulle, I can not say but I thought you ought to know of it.

A week from today is probably the most important election in our History.

That you will win I am certain, and that, by a majority that will amaze you.

You have no idea how much the people of Turkey and the minorities are hoping and praying for your election. In all the world I believe only the Germans and the Japanese hope for your defeat.

Cordially and respectfully yours,

George H. Earle[174]

The FDR Naval Aide File contains an intriguing entry that points to a document missing from the file. On November 1, 1944,

FDR sent a note to Admiral Wilson Brown asking, "What do you think of this?" A typed notation beneath FDR's question reads: "Letter to the President, 9-23-44, from Lt. Comdr. George H. Earle, U.S.N.R., Naval Attaché, American Embassy Istanbul, Turkey, suggesting that he (Earle) be sent to Germany on an American Mission – to continue personal observations and report conditions in Germany to the President." A handwritten note beneath the description of Earle's letter reads, "(Adm. Brown answered this direct + copy of reply is in files.)" This may refer to Earle's repeated attempts to get into Germany with the advancing American forces following the Normandy D-Day landings.

On December 9, 1944, once again Earle forwards a lengthy analysis on the post-war Russian question to FDR. He wrote:

Istanbul, 9 December 1944

My dear Mr. President:

The most vital question for world civilization is the future attitude and action of Russia. In other words "has the leopard changed its spots."

I enclose an article on this subject just written by a man of Russian and Polish blood who has lived many years in Russia, and who is thought by many here to be an excellent authority on Russia. I thought you might find it interesting.

Cordially and respectfully yours,

/s/

George H. Earle[175]

The President
The White House

The attached, 11-page, single-spaced, analysis, titled: "The Return to Tradition in Soviet Russia and The Future of Bolshevism," is a dense historical, sociological and political treatment of how the communists would adapt and manipulate traditional Russian themes to advance the party's agenda, and embrace apparently contradictory policies with an overriding objective of the ends justifying the means.

We do not possess an archival record of all of Earle's reporting from Istanbul. Records are missing and incomplete. In some instances, as we shall see when discussing the Katyn Forest Massacre, Earle's reporting was ordered "suppressed." However, what we are able to examine from existing files is a fascinating collection of reports and correspondence that shows the depth and scope of Earle's reporting network, his sense of the intelligence requirements he was collecting against, Earle's sense of urgency, and his "long view" to the post-war challenges facing the United States, particularly with respect to the Soviet Union and the geopolitical consequences for Western Europe.

Earle was not alone in his bitter criticism of the Soviet Union. His friend and colleague, Bill Bullitt was sounding the same alarms, as was John C. Wiley, a Soviet expert with the OSS whose recommendations to FDR mirrored Earle's in remarkably similar language and suggestions.[176]

Chapter 11

"The Earle Case"

While the National Archives files on George Earle's tenure as presidential emissary and Assistant Naval Attaché in Istanbul are incomplete – there is one file of particular interest that has not been previously examined and discussed. The collection of foreign embassy communications intelligence intercept cables, from February 1944 to December 1944, are assembled under a business-sized envelope bearing the official US government stationary mark "The White House" and bearing the title: "TOP SECRET DATA RE EARLE CASE."[177]

Eight pages of intercepted foreign diplomatic cable communications are in the file. They were classified (varyingly) from Top Secret to Secret and described the status and actions of Earle in Istanbul to foreign governments. This file is significant, because it is material evidence that within the FDR administration, someone thought to create a "case" regarding Earle and access the most classified intelligence collection capabilities of US intelligence to keep track of him. We do not possess the Earle "case file" – just the foreign embassy intercepts – so we do not have context or perspective on the decision to open a case, other reporting, analysis or commentary, or when and how the case was ever closed. It is a very intriguing insight into how the FDR White House viewed and considered Earle, but it is also somewhat frustrating because of the anecdotal or snapshot view of each report. We do not have the FDR administration record for what drove the creation of "The Earle

Case." We are compelled to ask: Why did the FDR White House create a Top Secret intelligence case file on the man designated presidential emissary to the Balkans and the Assistant Naval Attaché?

The first Secret cable in the file is from February 5, 1944 and features the reporting of someone in the Greek embassy in Cairo named "Tsouderos" to the Greek embassy in London, relaying a report from their Consul in Jerusalem:

> From conversations with a friendly American colleague I have confirmed that the so-called 'Naval Attaché' in Istanbul, and lately United States Minister in Sofia, Earle, who is now in charge of allied political propaganda for Bulgaria, is on friendly terms with many leading Bulgarian military and political personalities, with whom –M-- developments in the Balkans; that in some of his reports he argues in favour of the Bulgarian viewpoint; that he is favoured by ROOSEVELT; and that he is a friend of the United States Consul-General here, who remarked, "Greek circles in Istanbul ought to get together more with EARLE."

Next in the Earle case file is a declassified Top Secret diplomatic cable dated March 6, 1944, from Japanese ambassador in Ankara, Sho Kurihara to the Ministry of Foreign Affairs in Tokyo. This cable is extraordinary for its classification but also because it was part of the "Purple" cipher – Japan's most secure system. The Japanese ambassador reported the following to Tokyo:

> EARLE, formerly American Minister at Sofia (now at Istanbul supervising activities in the Balkans), spoke as follows to a contact:

> The American Ambassador at Moscow had reported the view that the Red Army would not penetrate far to the west of the former 1939 frontier. This was at one with the wishes of President ROOSEVELT.

(?2?) [sic] It was to be regretted that, in spite of the fact that the establishment of a second front would be for Great Britain the parting of ways between life and death, the British had but little comprehension of this. Thus it was a fact that even on the Italian front there were, in addition to American forces, large numbers of Indian, Canadian and French troops relatively few United Kingdom troops, but it was expected that when it came to setting up the second front the British would endeavour to reduce as far as possible the numbers of their own troops employed, and it was disagreeable that the British in any case depended too much on America.

3. The British were very insistent on Turkey's entering the war, but he did not think that this would have much effect on the war situation, and there was no need to be flurried.

The Nationalist Chinese ambassador to Turkey (Tsou Shang Yu) reported in a Secret diplomatic cable to Chungking on March 6, 1944 that:

Intelligence from Turkish sources. The lack of harshness apparent in the Soviet peace terms to Finland is an artifice to ingratiate the U.S.S.R. with each of the smaller powers. The swing over toward the United Nations is on the point of becoming pronounced. SEVOFFA is still in Turkey. VALEF (?VULEFF?), a previous Bulgarian Minister of Commerce, has also arrived; I hear that he is already in touch with EARLE, former United States Minister to Rumania (?Bulgaria?).

TSOU SHANG YU

Also, on March 6, 1944, Japanese ambassador Sho Kurihara, personally reported via Berlin to Tokyo the following in a now-declassified Secret cable:

Recently in connection the negotiations concerning an armistice with Finland the enemy authorities have made much ado, for propaganda purposes, about the opening of negotiations with Bulgaria in regard to a separate peace.

According to what I have found out through my own private inquiries, the architect SEVOFF, who is at present staying in Ankara, has in fact been in touch with certain enemy officials. According to a government report from an official in the German Embassy here (our "HA" intelligence man), this man has first of all been in contact with the American Minister in Istanbul, EARLE, formerly Minister to Sofia. He has also, it seems, had a secret meeting with the American Ambassador, STEINHARDT. But because the Americans do not make clear what their stipulations were, his plan has fallen to the ground.

On the 3rd the newspaper CUMHURIYET reported a rumor concerning the man's secret schemes. Recently, it would seem, this person has accepted the views of the Turkish Government circles. Since the collapse of Anglo-Turkish negotiations the Turkish authorities have looked with disfavor on any such schemes as these on the part of the various Balkan countries.

The newly appointed Russian Minister and others have also tried such schemes in Istanbul, we have been informed. MENEMENCIOGLU, the Foreign Minister, has recently heard in regard to these actions that since Turkey desired tranquility and stability in the Balkans she would like to see Rumania at this time, despite the change in the war situation, tighten her relations with Germany and oppose the projects of the Red Army. He was indirectly warning against this sort of activity when he made this pronouncement, I think.

The next Top Secret Japanese cable from Ankara to Tokyo in the "Earle Case" is dated September 5, 1944 and reports specific language that appeared in a March 1944 letter from Earle to FDR. Kuirhara reported:

At the end of last month BERGERY, the former French Ambassador, told me that, according to a statement made to him in confidence by a person in close touch with ROOSEVELT (he said he was an influential personage who had recently visited Turkey but he could not disclose his name), the view was strongly held in American political circles that the continuation of the war against Germany was nothing but a transfer of Europe from one gangster to another and that it was folly to shed the precious blood of American youth in a war of this kind, and that this view was gradually having an effect upon public opinion. And according to reliable information Minister EARLE (head of the American organization in the Balkans) takes exactly the same line, and, asking doe whose sake it is that America is active in the Balkans, says that the whole thing is senseless and evinces great dissatisfaction with the actions of the U.S.S.R.

Specifically referencing the cable above, Kurihara wrote another cable to Tokyo on October 21, 1944 – and, again, American Army cryptographers at Arlington Hall Station in Virginia intercepted and decrypted the Top Secret "Purple" diplomatic code. Kurihara wrote:

> Reference my telegram No. 415.
>
> A secretary of the Spanish Legation here gave the following information to a member of my staff. The American Minister EARLE, stationed at Constantinople (Head of the American organization in the Balkans), remarked some days ago to the Spanish Minister that the European situation was getting into an uncontrollable mess as "The cat that ate the cheese having been killed they were pursued by an innumerable swarm of rats," and said that he himself was repeatedly advising President ROOSEVELT in strong terms on the question of the Bolshevization of Europe. The Spanish Minister got the impression that EARLE was in favor of establishing touch with Germans without delay. Repeated to Berlin.

The last diplomatic cable in the Earle Case is a declassified Top Secret message from Spanish Minister Rojas in Ankara to the Ministry of Foreign Affairs in Madrid, dated December 5, 1944. Rojas wrote:

Mr. EARLE, the personal delegate of the President of the
United States, tells me that he has received instructions to
be ready to undertake a journey to Germany without
details as to the place or method of getting there. It is his
wish to go to America first for a thorough exchange of
views. He informed me that the anti-Russian party in the
United States grows daily, and that the President himself
bears in mind the Soviet dangers even if – G — necessities
of the war force him to temporize and not dispense with
help that is so valuable for the moment. A French doctor
who knows De GAULLE personally said that this
progressive – G – (?was due to him?). The informer who,
a month in advance, told him (EARLE) about the V.1.
raids, now assures him that V.3 aimed at America will
come into operation before the end of the month.

Reviewing these diplomatic cables, one can deduce the FDR
White House's interest for creating the "Earle Case." Naturally,
foreign governments would be interested in the activities and
comments of FDR's personal emissary. Earle had sufficient
standing, credentials, experience and contacts to merit that, simply
based on his appearance in Istanbul. The diplomatic cables bring out
other points to consider. No doubt the "gangster" language found in
Earle's March 1944 letter and the September 1944 Japanese cable
(focusing on the discussions with Vichy French diplomat Bergery)
drew White House attention – as well as criticisms of the Soviet
Union, which were not well-received given FDR's sympathies
towards Stalin and the documented, multiple successful penetration
of the administration by the N.K.V.D.

Lastly, there may have been a lingering question dating back
to the Canaris and von Papen initiatives (that began in January 1943)
to turn over Hitler and arrange an armistice with the Western Allies
aimed at the ultimate defeat of the Soviets. How far had Earle gone?
Were there contingency plans? Had negotiations been suspended?
Had the successes of the Normandy Invasion in June 1944 created a

renewed sense of urgency or desperation on the part of the German Resistance?

While we do not possess the full "Earle Case" file through the holdings of archives, the diplomatic communications intercepts provide us with an intriguing glimpse into the backstory of how the FDR White House kept tabs on the intrigues of Istanbul.

Chapter 12

Emissary on Thin Ice
May 1944 to March 1945

The Earle Case file takes on new meaning when one considers the messages the Presidential Emissary to the Balkans was conveying back to the FDR White House. Earle was not reporting ideas and facts popular with FDR and his staff.

It took the Russians forty-seven years (in 1990) to finally admit the criminality of the Soviet regime slaughtering approximately 22,000 Poles in the Katyn Forest. That level of denial was manifest in the FDR White House.

In May 1944, Earle traveled to Washington DC to see FDR. In an August 1958 magazine article Earle recalled his White House meeting:

> In the White House ante-room, waiting to see the President, I talked with Secretary of the Navy James Forrestal. It was five years before his tragic suicide would shock the world. I told him my fears of Russia.
>
> 'My God, George,' he said, 'you and I and Bill Bullitt are the only ones around the President who know the Russian leaders for what they really are.'
>
> But the President was relaxed and full of confidence. 'Stop worrying, George. We are getting ready for this Normandy landing. It cannot fail. Germany will surrender in a few months.'
>
> 'Mr. President,' I said, 'the real menace is not Germany. It is Russia.'

FDR smiled. George, Russia is a nation of 180 million people speaking 120 different dialects. When the war is over, she will fly to pieces like a cracked centrifugal machine at high speed.[178]

Earle went on to make his case – that the Soviets were responsible for the Katyn Forest Massacre – to the President with photos, affidavits, Red Cross reports, autopsy documents, and interviews Earle conducted with his extensive network of Central and Eastern European contacts. Earle's conclusion, that the Soviets had slaughtered the Poles, was rejected and his reporting suppressed.[179] FDR did not want to hear Earle's analysis and conclusion. Earle pressed on, and told FDR anyway. Ever respectful of the office of the Presidency and his old friend, Earle persisted, nonetheless.

Earle testified to Congress (in 1947 and 1952) that FDR was predisposed to ignore the evidence, stating: "George this is entirely German propaganda and a German plot. I am absolutely convinced the Russians did not do this." Earle rebutted that the evidence was overwhelming.[180] FDR did not find Earle's evidence and argument persuasive. He returned to Istanbul, until February 1945 when he requested to reassignment back to the United States.

Back in Philadelphia a month later, Earle was met with a divorce petition from his wife Huberta. He took up residence in the Racquet Club and considered his next moves.

Earle decided to attempt another meeting with FDR. As fate would have it, Earle received a telegram from FDR's personal assistant, William D. Hassett, asking him to come to the White House for an appointment with the President on Monday (March 19, 1945).

Earle, running a fever, took a sleeper train from Philadelphia to Washington DC's Union Station Sunday evening, and then taxied to the White House to see his old friend, the President. But upon arrival, Earle was rebuffed by FDR myrmidons and told the

President was too busy. He returned to Philadelphia and his rooms at the Racquet Club unheard.

In reviewing Earle's comments on this particular trip, and the writings of the handful of others who have discussed it, one is left with a sad, poignant feeling of "how the mighty had fallen."

Context and perspective are critical at this juncture. Consider: The man who earned a battlefield commission chasing Pancho Villa, and was awarded the Navy Cross in World War I; the 1940 Democratic presidential "heir apparent" who had made political room (and written large checks) for FDR to run for an unprecedented third term; the Governor of a crucial northeastern industrial state with groundbreaking credentials in support of workers and civil rights; the experienced and connected diplomat who placed himself in grave personal jeopardy in both Vienna and Sofia; the critical human channel for an early armistice ending World War II and confronting the Soviet menace; the man trusted to be the eyes and ears of the President in a critical neutral city of geopolitical significance – that man was sent packing from the White House without even the courtesy of a 15-minute office call.

The FDR White House of March 1945 clearly appreciated other points of view than those offered by Presidential Emissary Earle. *De rigueur* now was what Forrestal and Bullitt had warned Earle about – the Stalinist influence and hard Left tilt of Hopkins and several others. The Yalta Conference of February 4-11, 1945 had (just 3 months earlier) redrawn the map of Europe – with FDR (via Alger Hiss) conceding swaths of Eastern Europe in what would become the Warsaw Pact to the Soviets. The same Soviets who had invaded Poland at the same time as their then-allies, Nazi Germany. Only, thanks to Yalta, rather than Soviet leaders being put on trial for "waging a war of aggression" the Soviets would, instead, have a judge on the tribunal to judge the Nazis. The historical irony is quite rich, but rarely mentioned, and almost never discussed meaningfully. All this disturbed Earle deeply.

It was also painfully obvious that Earle was "one of those" who was not "up to speed" with how the brave new world had been arranged and designed at Yalta. Earle was a dinosaur from another, bygone, age. An FDR "old boy" who was just too old, now. He clearly did not truly or accurately understand the real history they were now writing, and besides, he had spoken to Germans during the war. "Everyone" knew what that meant.

Back in his Philadelphia Racquet Club rooms, Earle contemplated how to bypass FDR's handlers and gatekeepers. This is the George Earle of conviction. The moment and circumstance when a man of action faces a crisis of conscience. The man discussed in the introduction to this work. The true believer. The man whose 93-year old son said, "He would do any damn thing he felt like!"

George Earle wrote to the President's daughter – Anna Roosevelt Boettiger – who also assister her father with certain administrative duties in the White House. Earle's approach was brilliant and effective. It may have been "too" effective, as we shall see – but Earle hit his mark and communicated his message, loud and clear. That is how George Earle operated.

Chapter 13

Confrontation: Exile of the Emissary

Samoa is a very great distance from Washington, DC. It is more than 7,000 air miles. George Howard Earle III was exiled there. He may have been Governor of Pennsylvania at one time, but in the interests of the United States Navy, he was reduced to "Assistant Military Governor and High Sheriff of American Samoa."[181]

It started with a letter composed by Earle to Anna Boettiger on March 21, 1945. The letter was a device to end-run FDR's handlers and staffers who viewed Earle as too troublesome or too unimportant to gain either the attention of or access to the President. Thankfully, we have the entire text of the letter:

> The Racquet Club
> Philadelphia
> March 21, 1945
>
> Dear Mrs. Boettiger:
>
> You may remember I wrote to you about the Sultan Mohammed IV hunting knife I had for your father. I told you I would like to give it to your father personally but if he were too busy I would send it to you to give to him. Then I had a telegram from Mr. Hassett asking me to come to Washington Monday that the President wanted to see me personally.
>
> Sunday I got out of bed with a fever of 103, took a sleeper to Washington to be on time and called Mr. Hassett as to the exact time for the appointment and was informed by

him the President was too busy to see me and would I stop by the White House and leave the knife. So I am sending it to you to give to him.

The dates of the Sultan's reign are 1640-1692 and I consider it the finest Turkish antique I have ever seen. On the point and of the scabbard is the Sultan's turban, the stars on the blade are his personal motif, and his name in small Arabic letters are on two places on the scabbard.

As you may know my support of your father began in July 1932, about as early as a Republican could support him. Under him I have been Minister to Austria, Governor of Pennsylvania, Minister to Bulgaria, and three years in the U.S. Navy, the last two as Asst. Naval Attaché' in Turkey, reporting directly to him on Eastern Europe and Near East conditions. I have had several letters from your father congratulating me on my work.

Last autumn I felt my usefulness as an observer in that theatre was finished, so I wrote asking your father to transfer me to occupied Germany for some sort of work. Imagine my shock when I arrived here to find myself about to be brushed off to the inactive list and not sent to Europe for what Admiral Brown had been frank enough to say on several occasions was because of my anti-Russian attitude. In other words, because I told your father the truth about conditions in Russia and countries occupied by Russia, that near-Bolshevist group of advisors around the President had persuaded him to force me out of the picture.

However, before I am out of the picture, unless your father objects I want to present the following to the members of Congress and to the America people.

First, I shall tell of my opportunities for observation of the Bolshevists, their methods and results obtained, as Minister to Austria, to Bulgaria and two years as Asst, Naval Attaché' in Turkey reporting directly to the President. Then I shall recall my vigorous fight against Nazism from the very beginning in Austria in 1933, Bulgaria, etc.

Then I shall point out why Russia today is a far greater menace than Germany ever was, because of millions of unpaid fifth columnists. I shall show how Russia twenty-five years after its Revolution is exactly Red Terror it was then, of its 15 million people in concentration camps, of its treatment of the Jews and of Labor. I shall prove how Stalin deliberately started this war with his pact of friendship with Hitler so that the capitalist nations would destroy each other. I shall show the history books of 1944 being taught the Russian children, teaching Lenin's doctrines more strongly than ever, among which is stressed deceit, lie, treachery or murder is ethical if it helps the proletariat. I shall show how Mr. Davies and other high government officials were shown and heard of Russia only what the Bolshevist leaders wanted them to hear and see, as contrasted with me who interviewed scores of refugees.

I shall not do this until my papers have been received retiring me from active service, which I understand will be within the next week, and unless I hear from you, your father does not want me to do it.

I am no Raymond Moley or even Bill Bullitt. No matter how hurt I may be because your father resents the fact I told him the truth and after twelve years wants me to return to civil life, I shall never do anything to hurt or embarrass him as long as we both live.

I forgot to say that if I send this letter to the Press and members of the Congress, I shall ask a delegation be sent immediately to investigate the Russian breaking of promises in the Balkans, where they are sentencing to jail Bulgarian democrats who used to meet me secretly to plan opposition to Nazi influence and power in Bulgaria. I shall also state that the criticism of my article as being untimely or unpatriotic can hardly be considered so when from the bottom of my heart I believe the ally we are aiding will be a far greater menace to us and to civilization than the enemy we are now fighting.

If I do not hear from you in a week, I shall understand the President has no objection to me sending this letter to members of Congress and the Press.

Very sincerely yours,

George H. Earle[182]

One can imagine the look on FDR's daughter's face as she read Earle's letter. We have Anna Boettiger's forwarding note to what appears to be FDR assistant Grace Tully, and a brief glimpse at the immediate reaction within the White House. The short, typewritten note in the archives reads:

Dear Grace: This is Geo. Earle's present to Father which Earle says belonged to Sultan Mohammed the fourth. He says further: "The dates of the Sultan's reign are 1640 to 1692, and I consider it the finest Turkish antique I have ever seen. On the pointed of the scabbard is the Sultan's turban, the stars on the blade are his personal motif, and his name in small Arabic letters are on two places on the scabbard."

This is part of that terrible letter he wrote me, and which I read to you. Adm. Brown insists on seeing Father about this last. So, perhaps a letter of thank: [sic] had better wait until it is decided what to do about the gent.   Anna [signed][183]

FDR responded to Earle on March 24, 1945. The original letter, bearing the President's signature, is archived with the Historical Society of Pennsylvania in Philadelphia. It reads:

The White House
Washington
March 24, 1945

Dear George,

I have read your letter of March 21st to my daughter Anna and I have noted with concern your plan to publicize your unfavorable opinion of one of our allies at the very time when such publication from a former emissary of mine might do irreparable harm to our war effort. As you say, you have held important positions of trust under your Government. To publish information obtained in those positions without proper authority would be all the greater betrayal. You say you will publish unless you are told before March 28th that I do not wish you to do so. I not only do not wish it/but I specifically forbid you to publish any information or opinion about an ally that you may have acquired while in office or in the service of the United States Navy.

In view of your wish for continued active service, I shall withdraw any previous understanding that you are serving as an emissary of mine and I shall direct the Navy Department to continue your employment wherever they can make use of your services.

I am sorry that pressure of affairs prevented me from seeing you Monday. I value our old association and I hope that time and circumstances may some day permit a renewal of our good understanding.

Sincerely yours,

[Signed]

FRANKLIN D. ROOSEVELT.[184]

Commander George H. Earle, U.S.N.R.,
The Racquet Club,
Philadelphia, Pa.

The gravity and potential jeopardy of FDR's reply was not lost on Earle. He exercised the Anna Boettiger channel once again, in an effort to communicate directly with the President, writing: "Will you be kind enough to give the enclosed letter to the President? I assure you it will be the last time I shall bother you."

Earle's March 26th letter to FDR, via the President's daughter, stated:

The Racquet Club
Philadelphia

My dear Mr. President:

I have your letter of March 24. Your order as my Commander-in-Chief I shall obey to the letter.

Further than that, my gratitude for the honors you have conferred upon me and made possible for me compels me to give you my word of honor that I shall issue no public statement of any kind again as long as you are the President, except should you again decide to be a candidate when I shall certainly do all in my power in Pennsylvania to have you reelected.

Your friendship for me has been one of the most valued possessions in my life. When I wrote you that last letter I realized it might cost me that friendship. You may know, therefore, when I deliberately took such a risk how intense and sincere were my feelings and convictions.

On March 3, you wrote me that you thought a bigger field of usefulness lay before me in civil life. With those words you destroyed my desire to stay in the Navy.

Since nothing has occurred since those words of yours except that I should have had a difference of opinion with you (the first in thirteen years of association), I request respectfully that I be transferred to inactive duty.

May God give you health and guide you right in this Russian mess.

Very respectfully yours,

George H. Earle[185]

Hardly a surprise, but FDR would get the last word:

March 29, 1945

Dear George,

Your letter of March 26th has just reached me and your orders to duty in the Pacific have already been issued. As

I have already changed instructions once, I think you had
better go ahead and carry them out and see what you think
of the Pacific war as one of our problems.

With all good wishes,

Sincerely,

FRANKLIN D. ROOSEVELT[186]

Commander George H. Earle, U.S.N.R.,
The Racquet Club,
Philadelphia, Pa.

What an extraordinary exchange of personal letters! They
span matters stretching from the nature of Allied relations; the
looming threat of the Soviet Union; First Amendment freedoms;
Congressional and press oversight; national security; political
allegiance; old friendships; and personal vendetta in the extreme –
the banishment of an old personal friend and emissary to the far side
of the planet to ensure silence.

The subjects covered – frankly and rapidly by both parties –
are loaded with facts and layered meanings. Earle was fed-up and
determined to warn FDR, again, of his assessment of the real threat
posed by the Soviets. He would not be ignored or put off. He
distrusted the circle around FDR. Perhaps he saw FDR fading
physically and mentally, as others had observed and commented
upon? One thing was certain – Earle's conviction on the facts caused
him to craftily communicate around FDR's gatekeepers and get the
President's attention.

Earle's letter to Anna could not have been any franker and
more descriptive concerning his direct observations, interviews and
experiences. He laid out in no uncertain terms exactly what he was
going to do. All that he said was anathema to FDR. Then, to top it
all off, Earle gave the President of the United States one week to
respond to what amounted to an ultimatum – and some might call a

threat. There may not be any other comparable exchange in all the archives of presidential records.

Once FDR forbade Earle "to publish any information or opinion about an ally that you may have acquired while in office or in the service of the United States Navy," we get another insight into the character and strength of George Earle. Earle knows he is in very grave trouble. That his strong opinions and bold (some would say reckless) initiative had landed him in a position where he was not just controversial or unpopular but viewed as a threat by the President. He had crossed many, many lines before in his personal and professional life – but this situation was like none other.

How does Earle respond? Explicit obedience; gratitude and honor; friendship and honesty; a respectful request; and a closing prayer that sustains his warning to the President. It is an extraordinary letter. Earle respects the gravity of his personal and political jeopardy, seeks relief while reminding FDR of context, and still never backs off his warning. The letter reveals a lot about Earle the man in the same way FDR reveals much about his own character in his "last word" letter to Earle.

FDR's letter of March 29th is vindictive, disingenuous and petty. It shows the lengths the leader of the free world would go to crush an old friend. An old friend who had pledged obedience and sought to remove himself from the diplomatic and naval field. FDR's letter reeks petulant condescension and vengeful punishment. The reader knows full well that Earle could have been moved to the inactive rolls and sent home to Philadelphia with a few words muttered to one of FDR's naval aides.

What would motivate FDR to act this way towards Earle? How did it make FDR better, or stronger? What did it do for the country and the overall war effort? Was it really all about crushing someone who dared to tell him things FDR did not want to hear? Was there some lingering resentment that Earle had bankrolled

FDR's 1932 campaign and delivered Pennsylvania, one of the most important electoral victories that November? That FDR did not want to ever be reminded that he "owed" Earle? That Earle paved the way for FDR's unprecedented third term run in 1940 by preemptively getting out of the way – was something behind that? One must always remember: Earle did not need FDR.

In 1945, transferring a 55-year old "friend" more than 7000 miles away and into an active war zone to "see what you think of the Pacific war as one of our problems" is outrageous on any scale. In the alternative, if one wishes to ensure exile and isolation than Samoa appears to be the answer.

FDR's smug satisfaction at exiling Earle would be but a brief two weeks. The President died on April 12, 1945.

Earle would survive his brief stay on Samoa. His son, Lawrence Earle, an Army lieutenant assigned to the OSS but detached as a general's aide would "borrow" an airplane and fly 2250 miles from Bougainville Island to visit his father for a few days. By June, Earle was clamoring to return to the United States. He was back by July.

Samoa seems to have emboldened Earle, if that were even possible. His personnel file reads as though his return from Samoa was tied to an immediate separation from the Navy – but then there is a dramatic change in the paperwork. Earle begins communicating with admirals in the Navy's Bureau of Personnel, "Bupers," about the Naval Attaché job in Cairo, but he's willing to take anything in "a country in Europe or the Near East."[187]

In late October 1945, Earle writes to Bupers:

> Should it be a Mediterranean country, I have a small yacht with two diesel engines which is built primarily for seaworthiness and which I believe could live through almost any storm. I shall operate it at my own expense. With this yacht I can drop in at places not otherwise easily

reached, and it is in some of these smaller places where valuable information is sometimes obtained.[188]

This paragraph is "classic Earle" and so grossly far outside the scope of conventional Navy personnel assignment thinking as to be hilarious. In closing, he notes that his terminal leave expires November 28, 1945, strongly suggesting that the personnel staff should get busy finding him his next assignment.

In early November 1945, Earle took leave and traveled to Europe aboard the *USS Lake Champlain*. Earle was is not-so-secretly enroute to Istanbul and his love, the 23-year old beauty, Jacqueline Sacre, the daughter of a Belgian engineer advising the Turkish national railway. Jacqueline was born in Paris and educated in French and Istanbul convents. Along the way, Earle managed to have himself called back onto active duty on December 5, 1945 and appointed the Naval Attaché in Cairo.

All was not well in Cairo, as the personnel record for Earle contains his cable message of December 28, 1945 stating: "Refuse accept insulting subordinate appointment Cairo. Cancel immediately my orders active duty otherwise accept my resignation naval reserve. George Earle."[189]

Earle went beyond a personnel cable to the Navy. He sent a cable to President Harry Truman as well. It read:

> Have refused insulting subordinate appointment offered by Navy Department to Cairo and offered my resignation Naval Reserve. Believe this result of Regular Navy clique. Upon my return from Samoa, I used pressure to have Regular Navy governor of Samoa removed due to his sadistic treatment of natives. Wish you another successful year.
>
> Signed: George Earle[190]

The Navy was keenly aware of the cable to Truman and sought to reach Earle in Istanbul to grant the cancellation of his orders and his separation from active service.

It appears that Earle hoped to return to Istanbul, marry Jacqueline, and then spend time on his yacht, sailing around the Mediterranean and honeymooning. We do not have a record of what transpired in Cairo, but it is clear from Earle's cables that things did not develop as he had planned.

Earle and Jacqueline married on Friday, December 28, 1945 in a civil ceremony at a municipal building in Istanbul. A religious ceremony followed at the US Consulate with the Rev. Ezra Young, a Congregationalist from Pittsburgh, officiating. By the first week of January 1946, Earle's Navy orders were cancelled. The newlyweds sailed for the United States in March.

EARLE'S BRIDE — Former Jacqueline Saere, 23, a Belgian, is the bride of Comdr. George H. Earle, 55, former diplomat and one-time governor of Pennsylvania. They were married in Istanbul, Turkey, where Earle is stationed at American Embassy.

In September of 1947 the couple was blessed with a daughter, named for her mother. Earle was quoted in newspapers as being "delighted" with the arrival of his fifth child and first daughter.

Chapter 14

The Postwar Years

Consistent with his gubernatorial warnings to organized labor in the 1930s, as well as his intelligence reports to FDR dating back to 1943, George Earle was a fierce opponent of communism in all forms and the ambitions of the Soviet Union in particular.

Immediately upon returning to the United States, Earle took a bold strike at the Soviet Union. The *New York Times* reported in a March 23, 1946 article titled, "Earle Offers Russia Atomic Ultimatum:"

> Russia has made civilization's outlook the 'blackest in history,' George H. Earle, former United States Minister to Bulgaria and Austria, said today on his arrival here [Boston] from Istanbul, Turkey. He recommended using the atomic bomb against the Russians if necessary, if they refuse to retreat to their own territory and 'stop torturing other nations.'
>
> …
>
> He accused American statesmen of being 'Pollyannas' on the subject of Russia and said we were using the same appeasement tactics that were used with Hitler, but against a far greater threat to the democracies.
>
> 'Russia,' said Mr. Earle, 'has made a farce out of the United Nations Organization. Russia has hamstrung the UNO so that it cannot do anything. They are the ones who insisted on the veto power which took all the teeth out of the UNO. They have made the UNO a complete world joke and a farce.'[191]

Earle had barely returned to Philadelphia when the Nuremberg Trials raised questions about his communications with certain German officials in the *Widerstand* – the anti-Hitler resistance. In March 1945, former German Chancellor (and Vice Chancellor to Hitler) Franz von Papen, whom we remember as the German ambassador to Turkey during Earle's time as presidential emissary, made representations to the war crimes tribunal detailing overtures for peace that he initiated or conveyed.

Earle made statements to the major wire services and newspapers essentially confirming the peace feelers that von Papen was associated with. Earle went so far as to identify Baron Kurt von Lersner by name and to discuss the Germans' desire to keep their army intact under terms of an armistice with the Western allies in order to turn east and fight the Soviet Red Army in an effort to defend East Prussia, Poland, Czechoslovakia, Hungary and the Balkans. Thanks in part to Earle's forthright testimony and intercession, von Papen would only serve slightly more than three years in prison and was released in 1949.[192]

The apparent relentless march of communism – seen with Soviet aggression in Eastern Europe and around the world, as well as the impending "loss of China" to the communists was deeply troubling to Earle. He became President of the American Anti-Communist Association. The revelations of Soviet espionage penetrations in the FDR administration, at every level, have been controversialized and marginalized as a Red "Scare" – or cartoonishly simplified as a modern-day witch hunt with the term "McCarthyism." Both terms are masterful propaganda ploys to distract from the facts of Soviet successes in deeply influencing US foreign and defense policy beginning in 1933. Use of the terminology itself and the popular culture symbols and soundbites belies the truths exposed through the communications intercepts of

Soviet cables from Washington DC to Moscow known as the "Venona Decrypts," made public in 1996.

Earle knew firsthand what the Soviet threat was to the United States. His experiences, contacts and interviews from postings to Vienna, Sofia and Istanbul – as well as other official and personal travel – gave him a deep appreciation of the realities under communist oppression. His warnings to FDR were rejected. As noted previously concerning Earle's conversations with Bullitt and Forrestal – the views and policy positions in the FDR White House leaned extraordinarily hard over to the Left and in sympathy with Stalin and the Soviets. Earle made himself clear, again, in response to a question from a congressional committee looking into the Katyn Forest Massacre in 1952: "I think that the love and respect and belief in Russia in the White House and other quarters was just unbelievable."[193]

Earle became an activist and speaker in the public policy arena on the anticommunist front. For greater personal latitude in public engagement, he decided to resign from his position as President of the American Anti-Communist Association and mentioned that fact in passing in a letter to President Harry Truman. Nonetheless, his fierce brand of anticommunism did not fly with President Truman. On February 28, 1947, Truman wrote to Earle, "People are very much wrought up about the Communist 'bugaboo' but I am of the opinion that the country is perfectly safe so far as Communism is concerned—we have too many sane people."[194]

Earle's view of Soviet aggression and their race to develop an atomic bomb was quite grim. He gave interviews and public speeches describing the situation for the United States as "completely desperate." He believed that once the Soviets had developed their atomic weapon, they would not hesitate to use it, and that the United States stood as the only stumbling block to their plans for world domination. During sworn testimony before the House Committee on Unamerican Activities[iv] in March 1947, Earle recommended that America "immediately use the atomic bomb" against any nation that refuses to permit inspection of atomic plants – but also conceded that, "the American people wouldn't stand for it." He went on to explain, "This is a day of exaggeration for the sake of emphasis, of overstatement for dramatic effect."[195]

Earle was desperately trying to make a point. He knew, firsthand, what the Soviets had done in Eastern and Central Europe, and what they were capable of doing. He knew how compliant and sympathetic the FDR White House was towards the Soviets.

One small, yet chilling example of what compliance with Soviet demands for the Allies meant: Earle knew that American and British governments were engaged in the forced repatriation of Soviet (Yugoslav and Hungarian, too) prisoners of war back to the Soviet Union, irrespective of their wishes – and almost certainly to a Soviet labor camp or execution. The brutal repatriation campaign, dubbed "Operation Keelhaul," carried out by the US Armed Forces from August 1946 to May 1947, featured reports of Soviet mass suicide attempts at places like Fort Dix, New Jersey and soldiers from the 101st Airborne Division stuffing railcars in the Bavarian village of Plattling with 3000 Soviet soldiers for shipment to slave labor camps.[196] Is this what the Allies had fought for?

The context for Earle's statement was the March 1947 hearing dealing with a bill to outlaw the Communist Party. When pressed on that particular issue, Earle stated, "There is not the slightest question in my mind that Communist and fellow travelers

---

[iv] Misleadingly and repeatedly referred to as the "House Un-American Activities Committee" (HUAC) in a rhetorical propaganda victory for the Left – as that form and use of the name creates the impression that the House of Representatives had created a committee to engage in Un-American activities – *i.e.*, hold "witch trials," deny citizens their rights, etc. Control and manipulation of the popular lexicon was an oft-cited goal of the Italian Marxist Antonio Gramsci and implemented in America under Saul Alinsky's "Rules for Radicals."

in this country should be considered as agents of ruthless enemies bent upon our destruction."[197]

Following up on the earlier "bugaboo" letter to Earle, and Earle's congressional testimony, Truman was again compelled to respond. An April 4, 1947 *New York Times* article states, "President Truman has no fear that the Communist party will take over the American Government, he said today. He added that he was worried over persons owing allegiance to a foreign government holding public office in the Federal establishment."[198]

There is some political and rhetorical sleight-of-hand going on here that requires examination. Truman and Earle are in total agreement over deep concerns about persons owing allegiance to a foreign government. The news articles may not want you to think that – perhaps even Earle and Truman may not have wanted you to think that – but the very legitimate question of the day had to do with the penetration of Soviet agents, cooperators, "fellow travelers," and sympathizers into the "Federal establishment." The margin of difference here is that Truman is not willing to concede to Earle's characterization of the desperation of the situation.

Earle would not let up. By late April he was on the record in public discussions and speeches denouncing Stalin, "and what he called the 'murdering caste at the head of the Russian government.' Earle warned that Communist control of France would bring the Red threat nearer our shores. Earle pointed out that French Atlantic bases are located on St. Pierre-Miquelon and Martinique." [199]

In September 1947, Soviet Deputy Foreign Minister Andrei Vishinsky attacked Earle byname during a speech at the United Nations General Assembly. The *Associated Press* report detailed the bitterest portions of an "unprecedented blunderbuss," 8000-word address by Vishinsky naming Earle and eight other prominent Americans as "war mongers." One imagines Earle was quite pleased with himself.[200]

Close on the heels of the Soviet ministry, Carl Sandburg, the Lincoln biographer, decided to chime-in publicly and condemn Earle. During a literary festival at Coker College in South Carolina on October 6, 1947, Sandburg elected to associate himself with the remarks of Minister Vishinsky, and then doubled-down during an interview at his home in Flat Rock, North Carolina later that evening and amplify his remarks, warning, "that if the 'hate Russia' tide continues to rise the most terrible war in history is inevitable."[201] Sandburg's condemnation of Earle received broad notice by wire service syndication across the nation.

In February 1948, Earle testified before the House Committee on Foreign Affairs concerning "United States Foreign Policy for a Postwar Recovery Program." The focal point of the hearing was the Marshall Plan. Earle's introduction highlighted his extraordinary credentials and experiences and he, frankly, wandered and tarried a bit over the terrain concerning his warnings to FDR about the real threat posed by the Russians. That theme clearly weighed on Earle's mind because he was being asked to opine on the likelihood of success for a European recovery program that had the Soviet Union looming over it. Earle, seeming to be a contrarian, spoke frankly:

> I think this is a military situation and not an economic one ... With that situation over there, the fear the Russians at any time might move in, and the Communists in their own countries, not so great in numbers but in their fanaticism, and their organization tremendously strong, I feel that this is a military situation more than an economic situation. I feel that if we send dollars over there to Europe, without any military guaranty that that these Communists, who foment strikes and chaos, that our money will go to feed the people that are thrown out of work by these Communists in the strikes they bring about and that our money will just be tossed away ... If by any chance the Marshall Plan did start to succeed, I personally believe that Russia would simply occupy Europe ... There is one

other thing. I want to say to you gentlemen that Americans are great wishful thinkers. That is the thing I have had to fight since I was on this subject, on this crusade, trying to awaken our people to this great danger. They think that because of our magnificent American science perfecting a terrific atomic bomb the Soviet would not attack us because of fear of reprisal ... Admiral Zacharias said our bombs are now fifty times as powerful as those that bombed Hiroshima and Nagasaki. The Russians will have them some day without doubt. They are in possession of the German laboratory men, technicians, and mechanics and the finest raw materials in the world ...

About this Marshall Plan, I think the Europeans are very pessimistic, and very defeated and very low. I think if you had some kind of a military guaranty where Russia is concerned, to say to Russia if she takes one more foot of soil, it means war with the U.S., that might mean the stimulus they need. But I do not think that sending dollars over there with this fanatical, well organized Communist organization, fomenting strikes and using up our money to feed the people that cannot work, I really do not think that dollars alone will be enough. The Marshall plan will be a complete failure. That is what I think.[202]

The committee was scared, impressed and had more questions for Earle. Ohio Republican Congressman John Martin Vorys told Earle, "You have got us nearly scared to death, Governor. I want to say that I had the privilege of hearing you in an off-the-record talk at least 4 or 5 years ago, and your statements about the Russians were just the same in substance as to their intentions as you have stated today."[203]

Acting Committee Chairman Maloney asked Earle: "Now what is your thought in that respect, providing the Marshall plan is implemented by a strong military guaranty?"[204]

Earle answered Chairman Maloney stating:

Implemented by a strong military guaranty, absolutely, I am for it, 100 percent. But just dollars alone, with nothing to assure those people over there that we are going to back them up if Russia moves in, no.

Let me give you this as an example gentleman. I feel this very strongly. Let us suppose that the Russians occupied Canada with all their forces, and we had no Army, no Air Force, or Navy. Would you be interested in working hard to build up a business?[205]

Chairman Maloney spontaneously answered: "Naturally, I would not be." To which Earle replied: "There is the situation of every European country outside the iron curtain."[206]

Earle's instincts were correct. The economic recovery would require a military guarantee. The Marshall Plan required the North Atlantic Treaty Organization (NATO). The Marshall Plan operated for four years beginning on April 3, 1948. NATO was founded one year and one day later – on April 4, 1949.

Earle maintained his hard line on international inspections for nuclear, biological, chemical and radiological weapons. The Soviet's UN Security Council veto power frustrated him, and he even considered proposing an alternative structure to the UN. That entity would also flow from the creation of NATO – the North Atlantic Council – as the alliance's political structure in Brussels, Belgium. Earle seems to have been prescient in many respects. He may have articulated a hard line in a dramatic and occasionally exaggerated fashion, but his instincts were right.

By the autumn of 1948, with a November presidential election looming, Earle made an endorsement that reversed his political affiliation of nearly three decades. Philadelphia columnist John Cummings reported in the September 28, 1948 morning edition of the *Inquirer* that:

> Former Governor Earle, in the current presidential campaign is supporting the Republican nominee, Governor Tom Dewey. Although Mr. Earle was elected Governor of the State as a Democrat, he sees little if

anything, in the Truman record, to warrant the confidence of the American people. This, says Mr. Earle, is especially true of Mr. Truman's attitude towards the Communist issue ... The whole thing was a 'bugaboo' rather than a menace ... it is certain in the opinion of Mr. Earle, that our President hasn't the slightest idea of what the Communists are trying to do to the country. His repeated attacks on Senate and House committees investigating subversive activities, his refusal to provide the committees with information accumulated by the FBI, may be cited to prove the point made by the former Governor. Either he is ignorant of what is going on or he still nurses the idea he can wean the radical left wing vote away from Henry Wallace ... Governor Earle feels that if we had dealt firmly with the Russians in the first instance, if President Roosevelt had taken the devil by the heels when he saw him at Yalta, things would be different today. He sees neither hope nor prospect of firmness in Mr. Truman. So the man who was exiled to Samoa is supporting Governor Dewey.[207]

Truman's reelection did not slow down or diminish Earle's activism and advocacy. In November 1952, Earle provided sworn testimony to the United States House Select Committee to Conduct an Investigation of the Facts, Evidence, and Circumstances of the Katyn Forest Massacre. It was much the same testimony he provided the House Foreign Affairs Committee 4 years and 8 months earlier. Earle pointed that fact out to the committee in an effort to reinforce how long he had been reporting inconvenient and often ignored facts to the U.S. government on matters pertaining to the Soviet Union. He reminded the committee of FDR's behavior, the influence of Harry Hopkins and his "pink" (meaning, secretly "Red," or Communist) acolytes in the Administration – and that he had paid a personal price for telling the truth when it was unpopular and inconvenient.

Earle explained that upon FDR's death and his eventual
return from Samoan exile, *certain Truman administration officials
reached out to him:*

> When I returned from there [Samoa], the Chief of
> Personnel of the Navy and Commodore Vardaman, the
> President's Navy aide, both called me in to apologize to
> me and say they were very sorry, that the Navy
> Department had nothing to do with it.

> And then, Commodore Vardaman, one of Harry
> Truman's closest friends, made a very interesting remark.
> He said –

> We Truman people never turn over a Roosevelt stone that
> we don't find a snail under it.

> *I don't know what he meant by it, but possibly you
> gentlemen do. Now, I would like to go into this Katyn
> massacre.*[208]

Earle went on to explain his Katyn Massacre sources in
Istanbul. Among those sources: refugees, White Russians,
Bulgarian Red Cross officials, photographs, sworn affidavits and
other human intelligence-based reporting that corroborated the
details of the massacres of the Poles. He recalled how FDR reacted
and the scripted or "pat" response FDR gave to any unpleasant or
unwelcome news concerning the Soviets – that the country would
fly apart from internal domestic tension and division after the war.
Earle's testimony was not a "tough sell" to the committee members.
Many of them had open questions in their minds since the first
military attaché questions were raised in 1942.

Earle worked into his sworn testimony a piece of Soviet
propaganda that he found particularly offensive and a copy of which
he reportedly left with FDR in the White House. It was a large image
of the baseball player Babe Ruth with a baseball bat on his shoulder
and an adoring little boy looking up at the baseball hero. Underneath
the image, the Soviets had place the language, "Typical of

democratic America: this great American brute is about to club this little American boy to death."[209] He found it so outrageous and deceitful of our Soviet "ally" that he felt compelled to bring it to the attention of the committee and the general public even though it had no direct bearing on the massacre in Katyn Forest.

Trying to explain his understanding of the FDR White House approach to the Soviet Union, Earle stated:

> The liberal got all twisted up. They seemed to think that communism was liberalism, whereas, in reality, communism is the worst enemy of liberalism. There is no freedom of the press; no right of collective bargaining; no freedom of speech. It violates every tenet of liberalism.
>
> Yes; I think these Americans for Democraic Action should be called Americans for Socialistic Action.
>
> May I say the American people don't know the difference between socialism and communism. Let me tell you the difference. I am sure that many of you know it. The only difference is this: They both believe in Lenin's teaching. The only difference is that the Communists believe in seizing it by a militant minority, any kind of crime to get it, by violence, while the Socialists mean to get it by legal means or by the vote of the people. There is no difference. They both believe absolutely in the teachings of Lenin. There is no difference except in the method of attaining it. Very few people realize that.[210]

By the mid-1950s, Earle was dividing his time between homes in Coral Gables, Florida and Radnor, Pennsylvania. He had undergone one serious surgery for stomach ills in Philadelphia, and then returned to Florida for a time to recover. He became involved in the 1956 Florida campaign for Eisenhower and was a reliable political surrogate and fundraiser, and could always draw a crowd. The convictions of Alger Hiss, Harry Dexter White and Gregory Silvermaster – among others – validated Earle's warnings.

In 1958, Earle exchanged a series of letters with retired U.S. Army General Albert C. Wedemeyer who had just published his memoir, *"Wedemeyer Reports!"* Wedemeyer played a major role in Army planning as General George C. Marshall's chief of staff from the prewar period up through the Normandy invasion. He spent the latter portion of World War II as the China-Burma-India Theatre commander and then was assigned as Chiang Kai-shek's chief of staff. Wedemeyer was cut from the very same anti-communist cloth as Earle. Earle's handwritten letters from Radnor, PA in November and December 1958 to the General and his replies are mutual affirmations by men who had seen and lived a part of America's hidden history that they were finally able to explain and discuss freely.

Thanks to the Hoover Institution Archives, we have the exchanges between these two remarkable and overlooked American patriots. On November 7, 1958 Earle writes:

Dear General:

I am deeply touched and appreciative of your book, and the fine words you wrote.

The book is amazing and shocking, but every word rings true.

I am sending seven or eight copies to friends of mine including Otto of Austria, Franz von Papen, Duc de Nemours, the Queen of Bulgaria (sister of the last King of Italy).

I enclose copies of my testimony before certain committees of the Congress which are the only ones I have.

Would you be kind enough to register mail them when you return them at your convenience. I think after reading my debate with Chancellor Hutchison of Chicago University you may agree with me he certainly XXXX on being a fellow-traveler.

With kindest regards

Your friend,

/s/

George H. Earle [211]

Approximately three week later, Earle followed up:

Dear General:

I enclose my article in Confidential in 1952 or '53.

Forrestal was a personal friend of mine. After I returned from Samoa I asked him why he insisted I go to Samoa at the time of FDR's death. He replied he wanted more concrete evidence of FDR's fanatical love of Communist Russia & Samoa was a nice place to be for a few months.

Will you be kind enough to return this clipping and the others registered mail to me in a few days.

In confidence, do you feel Quemoy etc. are defensible? [Islands under the jurisdiction of Taiwan]

I have now sent twelve copies of your great book to friends. Be sure to get the Philadelphia Inquirer of Nov 23rd, (the second largest morning newspaper in the USA) for your books review.

Cordially,

/s/

George H. Earle [212]

General Wedemeyer replied to Earle on December 6, 1958:

Dear Governor:

Thank you so much for your note concerning my book. I know that the actual descend [sic] upon me as soon as the left wingers get over the impact. Unquestionably they're already preparing a whispering campaign to impute my motives or to smear my good name. Furthermore they will do everything possible to curb public interest in my book and to repudiate some of the truthful premises established between its covers. Fine Americans like you who are unafraid to tell the truth, unafraid of the truth, and unafraid to abide by the truth, will recognize the attacks for what they really are, but I fear that many of our gullible countrymen will be taken in.

Whenever I met an interesting person or experienced some unusual event, I made notes in over the years have kept them in rather crude form. These notes together with government or official records from archives formed the basis for the book. Of course the conclusions I have drawn are my own, but they are strongly fortified by men of goodwill, sincerity of purpose, and guts like yourself.

The last election would indicate that we are losing the battle but I intend to do my utmost to stem the tide and to perpetuate the opportunities that I knew as a boy for a wholesome and constructive life for succeeding young men and women.

All good wishes for your health and happiness. God bless you.

Faithfully,

A.C. Wedemeyer
General, U.S. Army (Ret.)

P.S. I am returning herewith registered, as requested, your very wonderful documents which I certainly enjoyed reading.

Thank you for making them available.

A.C.W.

Honorable George H. Earle
Radnor
Pennsylvania

Two days later, December 8, 1958, another letter from the General to the Governor:

Dear Governor:

I'm returning here with the interesting material concerning your experience with FDR. I don't quite understand Jim Forrestall's idea of placing you on the shelf in Samoa immediately after FDR's death. To me, Jim Forrestall was the epitome of patriotism and guts. I talked to him considerably while he was Secretary of Defense and found him to be in accord with truly American ideas and ideals.

If you have any evidence that I might use concerning FDR's efforts to ensure that we become active belligerents in World War II, this would be very helpful to me when the left wingers really bear down, which they inevitably will do.

You inquire about the defensibility of Quemoy and Matau [sic]. It is in my considered opinion that the Communists could capture Quemoy or Matau anytime they wished. All of the military advantage lies on the Communist Chinese side. I might add that Quemoy and Matau are not important to the Chinese Nationalist government nor to us in a military or economic sense. Actually those islands are a liability with reference to those facets of strategy. But psychologically, if we permit the Communists to take any area that is currently free, it would be a tragic defeat for the free world, not only in the Far East but also in the Middle East and even in Central Europe. In other words, we are not fighting for real estate – barren rocky islands – in the Formosa Strait but we are fighting for the principle of sovereignty, of appeasing ruthless aggression, of decency among nations.

Again, I feel privileged that fate has crossed our paths, and I hope that when you are in Washington you will contact me.

With all good wishes for a happy holiday season to you and all members of your family.

Faithfully,

A.C. WEDEMEYER

General, U. S. Army (Ret.)

Honorable George H. Earle
Radnor
Pennsylvania

The final archival letter we have from George Earle was written in the Governor's rounded, rolling script, on old, scratched-through Racquet Club stationary, to General Wedemeyer on December 11, 1958, from his home on Gulph Creek Road in Radnor:

Dear General:

Thanks a lot for your fine letters.

I enclose a clipping from John Cummings the Phila. Inquirer's great columnist.

In re my knowledge of the provocation of Japan by Roosevelt and Churchill, I was in Sofia at the time, and three weeks before Pearl Harbor I told several members of my Legation there that with the announcement of the embargoes of raw material by Great Britain and the US, Japan <u>must</u> go to war being unable to exist without them.

In re Forrestal who was friend of mine, I feel like he was beginning to break up mentally when I wrote him of my exile (worry over Russia). I felt I was perfectly safe in Samoa and that the longer I stayed there the more damning it would be for the pro Russians in our government in both the Truman and Roosevelt administrations.

Cedric Salter, a nephew of Baron Salter, (prominent in the British war effort), was a very close friend of mine and reporter for the Daily Mail in London.

He came to see me in Istanbul and told me had just had lunch with Colonel Thompson a former C.I.D. inspector and head of the "killing" branch of the British Intelligence in the Near East.

Salter said Thompson was furious because the Marquis Prat [Pedro Prat y Soutzo], Spanish ambassador, had changed his plans at the last moment for an automobile trip to Ankara on which Col Thompson had it planned to have him in an automobile accident and pushed over a cliff, as he was the worst enemy of the British in the Near East.

Then Thompson said, 'George Earle is the next worst enemy of the British, and I'm going to have him completely discredited by starting the rumor all over Turkey that he is importing hashish through the diplomatic pouch and selling it through a Persian agent of his in the Grand Bazaar!'

I reported this to Steinhardt, our ambassador in Turkey who immediately went to work and reported it to Washington. A day later he informed the British ambassador that Washington came back instantly and said if anything happened to me, it would mean the most serious XXX consequences.

Admiral Zacharias was also busy and went to the top British intelligence officer who informed him, "Earle was now safe! (3 days later)."

My hostility to the British consisted in trying to see that we got fair play in Turkey and the Balkans and not pushed out of the picture by the British. Steinhart is dead but Zacharias if you see him will confirm it. Kindest regards. Your book is the talk of the town.

/s/

George H. Earle [213]

This last of the institutional, archival, Earle materials is remarkable for the mention of the British intelligence plotting against Earle. Cedric Salter's revelations concerning the scheme of British Colonel Thompson – and the subsequent American furor over the targeting of Earle are stunning revelations. Earle had not mentioned them in prior speeches, testimony, or writing.

Why and how Earle felt comfortable revealing the story to General Wedemeyer on this occasion remains a mystery. Nonetheless, there is little or no reason to doubt the veracity of Earle or Salter. Further supporting the notion that there was tension between Earle and the British operating in Istanbul is the Earle report to the White House of September 3, 1944 (quoted earlier) wherein he does express his frustration with the British over their efforts to constrain U.S. influence in the Near East.

While there are stories of ill-will and rivalries between the British and US allies (one is reminded of the animosity between Patton and Montgomery) throughout World War II, the personal targeting of Earle by British intelligence in extraordinary. During an interview with Earle's son, Lawrence, on December 4, 2016, he stated that his father was in grave danger during his clandestine meetings with von Lersner (concerning the proposed anti-Hitler coup, armistice and defense of Europe from the Soviets) in the outskirts of Istanbul. Lawrence Earle stated that his father faced being run off the road in remote locations on a few occasions and was also shot at by unknown persons in connection with those clandestine meetings. Lawrence intimated that the British were as likely as any of the other parties in Turkey to have sought disruption or termination of his father's activities. George Earle continued, nonetheless, undaunted.

Earle's public engagement and activism throttled back following the election of Eisenhower to the presidency. Public mentions of the governor are mostly in the society pages, or newspaper feature articles discussing dog shows, charities, reunions, and the political aspirations of people that had served under Earle in years past.

In November 1966, Earle suffered a stroke and hospitalized. His recovery was slow and the toll on his overall health was steep. Just over two years later, in January 1968, he was hospitalized again. This time, nursing care was required, and Earle's lifestyle changed dramatically. The energetic, mischievous, take-on-the-world, George H. Earle III was to be a resident of the Bryn Mawr Terrace Convalescent Center for the last eight years of his life.

Pneumonia took Earle from this world on Monday, December 30, 1974. His obituary in the *Philadelphia Inquirer* traced his long record of public service. "When he was asked in 1963 how he would sum up his best accomplishments, he replied: 'Many people think the greatest achievement of my regime was starting the Turnpike (the Pennsylvania Turnpike, which became the first in the nation). I don't. I'm proudest of my laws on minimum wages and maximum hours. 'Also, I like to feel that whenever I made an appointment, the person's race, religion or color had nothing to do with it.'"214

Earle was survived by his wife, Jacqueline; five sons, George H. IV, Hubert P., Lawrence W., Ralph II, and Anthony Wayne; a daughter, Jacqueline; 15 grandchildren, and six great-grandchildren. He was 84 years old.

Epilogue

Context and Perspective

Men of conviction are hard to find. Courage is in short supply. Popularity is confused with substance and real achievement. Few today can imagine putting themselves at grave personal risk or exercising initiative without guidance or permission. Intellect and curiosity are viewed with either suspicion or derision. Risk is managed. The truth, if ever told, is done so very slowly. Leaps of faith are only taken with appropriate headgear, a body harness and signed waivers.

We have been introduced to a remarkable man: George Howard Earle, III. They do not make them like that anymore. Earle was a man of his convictions. He was fearless without being foolhardy. An advocate and patriot who was proud of his country and its interests, but not too proud to admit a mistake or wrongdoing. Earle was an idealist with a practical streak. A cheerful, optimistic, cynic who understood the realities of national and international politics as well as he did the Pennsylvania coal miner's need to earn enough money to feed his family. Earle was a man of privilege and wealth with understanding and empathy. He had a big heart and a sense of humor. He was not afraid to make a mistake, because he knew his intentions were good and true.

Earle's life was full. The adventures and controversies are not merely entertaining and informative – they provide us with opportunities to examine our own circumstances, priorities, and decisions. We can reflect on what we might have done in Earle's shoes. Would we run into the burning engine room of a ship loaded with fuel and ammunition? Would we put ourselves between mobs of Communists and Nazis in a foreign capital and make a direct appeal to the people for democracy? Would we challenge communists seeking to infiltrate labor unions while protecting workers rights? Would we be willing to launch state-wide civil rights reforms, protecting minorities, thirty years before the rest of the country? How about dealing with Germans claiming to be anti-Hitler resistance leaders and plotting a coup? Would we go to the President and tell him we are willing to personally be the go-between with the coup plotters? Do we possess the fortitude to later confront the same President and essentially call him either a liar, a fool, or both – and then bear the consequences, on our honor? Are we willing to be personally denounced by a Soviet minister in front of the United Nations General Assembly for daring to tell the truth? Those are the big events in Earle's life, but pause and consider the hundreds, perhaps thousands, of smaller decisions. Consider his character. Consider his conscience. Consider his conviction. Consider the life of the man.

Earle's life was complicated. He was not a saint. Thankfully, he never pretended to be one, either. However imperfectly, we can see through the long view, over the course of his life, that he sought to stand for what was right, to protect the weak and vulnerable, and to act courageously in fighting for freedom and the truth. He bravely and repeatedly placed himself in harm's way. He may not have been a model of personal virtue in all respects. We know he had an eye for attractive women, and that eventually his marriage to Huberta ended in divorce. Many marriages do. It is a fact of our society. Nonetheless, we can say with confidence that George Earle was a good man. He was a man of his word and a man of discretion who could be counted upon to hold his end of a bargain or a promise.

There are some loose ends to the story of George Earle. Certainly, not everything has been scrupulously documented. There are archives in Harrisburg and Philadelphia, Pennsylvania – but they focus on a narrow period. Likewise, that is so with the records at the National Archives. Some records that should be there were suppressed by FDR. FDR's Presidential Library is another matter. The German, Austrian and British archives all contributed something, too.

The British Archives help answer some questions about the mysterious and lovely Adrienne Molnar. We never really got a satisfactory resolution of her relationship with "Hefty," but we have reason to believe she played a role in the defection of Willi Hamburger and perhaps other German intelligence assets in Istanbul. We know of her attachment, perhaps merely of convenience, to Earle. We also know that she came to the attention of virtually every other intelligence service in Turkey. The British MI5, MI6, Home Office, Metropolitan Police and US Embassy files – totaling 35-pages – help us understand that, and even some of her postwar life. Adrienne survived the war and Istanbul. Her real first name was "Irma." She married an American with the last name of Hyde and became a naturalized U.S. citizen. By 1952, it was the judgment of the British that she was involved in intelligence work, probably as a courier but perhaps handling agents herself. The file does not speculate as to her employer. She claimed to be an actress living in Paris, and would not discuss her plans to return to the United States. Her passport contained stamps for "innumerable journeys to England, Germany, Switzerland, and Italy," that, "cannot be explained satisfactorily by the alien herself. She is a liar, attractive and intelligent."[215] "Adrienne" is lost to us in June 1953.

So, we are left to speculate. Not just on the fate of Adrienne, but on much larger questions. The questions we started with. What if World War II had ended eighteen months earlier in an armistice, and the *Wehrmacht* turned in unison with the Western Allies against the Red Army? What if the Soviet influence operations and espionage penetrations of the FDR White House had been blunted or even rolled back and exposed before they were ever implemented? What if there were no Cold War to freeze the world into a half-century long nightmare that cost the world thousands of lives and millions of persons' political imprisonment?

Now 75-years since the end of World War II, we have a slightly different perspective on that mighty struggle than even that held by one generation ago. Time grants us that privilege. Stories like those of George Earle come to the surface. Lost history is recovered. Archives are declassified. There is a form of "recovery" done to unearth facts and records. We gain a clearer understanding of the topography – the terrain walked by other men in night and fog. Our better understanding illuminates the possibilities. In some cases, "Court histories" are brushed aside. In others, the facts and details just become more grim.

We are all a little better off knowing George Earle.

Endnotes

[1] Earle, George H. "FDR's Tragic Mistake." *Confidential*, Aug. 1958.

[2] Roosevelt, Franklin D. Letter to Commander George H. Earle III. "Letter from Franklin D. Roosevelt." *George Howard Earle Papers* (Collection 3260). Philadelphia, PA: The Historical Society of Pennsylvania, March 24, 2018.

[3] Earle, *op. cit.*, page 56.

[4] Fischer, Benjamin B. "The Katyn Controversy: Stalin's Killing Field." *Studies in Intelligence*, 1999.

[5] *BBC News.* "Russia to Release Massacre Files." December 16, 2004. http://news.bbc.co.uk/2/hi/europe/4102967.stm.

[6] Philadelphia War History Committee. *Philadelphia in the World War, 1914-1919.* New York, NY: Wynkoop Hallenback Crawford Co., 1922. Google Books: https://books.google.com/books?id=nYhPAAAAYAAJ&lpg=PA277&dq=%22USS%20Victor%22&pg=PA277#v=onepage&q=%22USS%20Victor%22&f=false.

[7] USS Victor Deck Log, February 10, 1918, Records of the Bureau of Navy Personnel, Record Group 24; National Archives Building, Washington, DC.

[8] Naval History and Heritage Command. "Victor I (S. P. 1995)." Published February 17, 2016. https://www.history.navy.mil/research/histories/ship-histories/danfs/v/victor-i.html.

[9] Motorboat Magazine, "New 74-foot Naval Patrol Boat" *Motorboat*, July 10, 1917, pp. 23-24.

[10] USS Victor Deck Log, February 10, 1918, Records of the Bureau of Navy Personnel, Record Group 24; National Archives Building, Washington, DC.

[11] *Ibid.*

[12] Naval History and Heritage Command. "Victor I (S. P. 1995)." Published February 17, 2016. https://www.history.navy.mil/research/histories/ship-histories/danfs/v/victor-i.html.

[13] *Military Awards for Valor - Top 3,* U.S. Department of Defense, "Navy Cross Recipients, World War I, 1917-1919." Accessed 29 AUG 2017 at: http://valor.defense.gov/Portals/24/Documents/ServiceCross/NavyCross-WWI.pdf

[14] National Governors Association. "Governor George Howard Earle III." Accessed Aug. 29, 2017. https://www.nga.org/cms/home/governors/past-governors-bios/page_pennsylvania/col2-content/main-content-list/title_earle_george.html.

[15] Pennsylvania Historical and Museum Commission. "Governor George Howard Earle III." Aug. 25, 2015. http://www.phmc.state.pa.us/portal/communities/governors/1876-1951/george-earle.html.

[16] *Evening News* (Wilkes-Barre, PA). "Boniwell Arrives." May 7, 1934.

[17] Pennsylvania Historical and Museum Commission. "Governor George Howard Earle III." Aug. 25, 2015. http://www.phmc.state.pa.us/portal/communities/governors/1876-1951/george-earle.html.

[18] *Time Magazine.* "National Affairs: Labor Governor." July 5, 1937. http://www.historicnewtownsquare.org/wp-content/uploads/1937-TIME-article.pdf.

[19] *Ibid.*

[20] Curtin, G. B. "Why is the Doberman Pinscher a Success?" *Dogdom*, February 1922.

[21] Davies, Lawrence E. "A Political Star Rises in Pennsylvania," *New York Times*, November 29, 1936.

[22] Wilcox, Levi. "Local Polo Star to Play in Miami." *Philadelphia Inquirer*, January 5, 1925.

[23] Brownell, Will and Richard N. Billings. *So Close to Greatness: The Biography of William C. Bullitt*. New York, NY: Macmillan Publishing Co., 1988. 21.

[24] *Historical Society of Pennsylvania*. "Closed for Business: The Story of Bankers Trust Company During the Great Depression, George Howard Earle III." Sept. 5, 2017. http://digitalhistory.hsp.org/bnktr/person/george-howard-earle-iii.

[25] *Pittsburgh Press*. "George Earle Spent $141,099." Dec. 6, 1934.

[26] Office of the Historian, US Department of State. "George Howard Earle III (1890–1974)." Accessed: Sept. 12, 2017. https://history.state.gov/department history/people/earle-george-howard.

[27] Lawrence W. Earle, interview by author, Bryn Mawr, PA, Dec. 2016.

[28] Earle, George H. "The Minister in Austria (Earle) to the Secretary of State, Oct. 28, 1933." Telegram. In *Foreign Relations of the United States: Diplomatic Papers 1933, General*, Vol. I. Document 60. Washington, DC: United States Government Printing Office, 1950.

[29] Earle, George H. "The Minister in Austria (Earle) to the Secretary of State, Nov. 8, 1933." Telegram. In *Foreign Relations of the United States: Diplomatic Papers 1933, General*, Vol. I. Document 62. Washington, DC: United States Government Printing Office, 1950.

[30] Dodd, William E. "The Ambassador in Germany (Dodd) to the Secretary of State, Sept. 13, 1933." In *Foreign Relations of the United States: Diplomatic Papers 1933, General*, Vol. I. No. 141. Washington, DC: United States Government Printing Office, 1950.

[31] Earle, George H. "The Minister in Austria (Earle) to the Chief of the Division of Western European Affairs (Moffat), Vienna, Austria, Nov. 21, 1933." In *Foreign Relations of the United States: Diplomatic Papers 1933, General*, Vol. I. No. 123. Washington, DC: United States Government Printing Office, 1950.

[32] *United Press*. "US Envoy Urges Austria to Avoid Anti-Semitism." *St. Louis Star and Times*. November 15, 1933.1.

[33] Earle, George H. "The Minister in Austria (Earle) to the Chief of the Division of Western European Affairs (Moffat), Vienna, Austria, Nov. 21, 1933." In *Foreign Relations of the United States: Diplomatic Papers 1933, General*, Vol. I. No. 123. Washington, DC: United States Government Printing Office, 1950.

[34] Phillips. "Memorandum by the Under Secretary of State (Phillips), Feb. 1, 1934." In *Foreign Relations of the United States: Diplomatic Papers 1933,*

General, Vol. I. No. 611.6315. Washington, DC: United States Government Printing Office, 1950.

[35] *Evening News* (Wilkes-Barre, PA). "Democrats of Pennsylvania Select Slate." Feb. 1, 1934.

[36] Kliefoth, A.W. "The Chargé in Austria (Kliefoth) to the Secretary of State, Jan. 27, 1934." In *Foreign Relations of the United States: Diplomatic Papers, 1934, Europe, Near East and Africa.* Vol. II. No. 611.6315. Washington, DC: United States Government Printing Office, 1950.

[37] Kliefoth, A.W., "The Chargé in Austria (Kliefoth) to the Secretary of State, Vienna, Austria, Feb. 12, 13, 1934." In *Foreign Relations of the United States: Diplomatic Papers, 1934, Europe, Near East and Africa.* Vol. II. No. 17 and 18. Washington, DC: United States Government Printing Office, 1950.

[38] Hull, Cordell cablegram to US Chargé Alfred Kliefoth, Washington, DC, Feb. 15, 1934. "The Secretary of State to the Charge in Austria (Kliefoth), Feb. 15, 1934." In *Foreign Relations of the United States: Diplomatic Papers, 1934, Europe, Near East and Africa.* Vol. II. No. 7. Washington, DC: United States Government Printing Office, 1950.

[39] Earle, George H. cablegram to Secretary of State Cordell Hull, Vienna, Austria, Feb. 28, 1934. In *Foreign Relations of the United States: Diplomatic Papers, 1934, Europe, Near East and Africa.* Vol. II. No. 37. Washington, DC: United States Government Printing Office, 1950.

[40] Hull, Cordell telegram to George H. Earle III, Washington, DC, Feb. 28, 1934. In *Foreign Relations of the United States: Diplomatic Papers, 1934, Europe, Near East and Africa.* Vol. II. No. 11. Washington, DC: United States Government Printing Office, 1950.

[41] Earle, George H. telegram to Secretary of State Cordell Hull, Vienna, Austria, March 2, 1934 In *Foreign Relations of the United States: Diplomatic Papers, 1934, Europe, Near East and Africa.* Vol. II. No. 39. Washington, DC: United States Government Printing Office, 1950.

[42] Kliefoth, A.W. "The Chargé in Austria (Kliefoth) to the Secretary of State, Feb. 16, 1934." In *Foreign Relations of the United States: Diplomatic Papers, 1934, Europe, Near East and Africa.* Vol. II. No. 23, 18. Washington, DC: United States Government Printing Office, 1950.

[43] Earle, George H. letter to Engelbert Dollfuß, March 23, 1934. Austrian State Archives.

[44] *Daily Republican* (Monongahela, PA). "Envoy Ordered Back." February 16, 1934. 1.

[45] Beers, Paul D. *Pennsylvania Politics: Today and Yesterday.* University Park, PA: Penn State University Press, 1980. 122.

[46] Keller, Richard C. *Pennsylvania's Little New Deal.* New York: Garland Publishing, 1982. 398.

[47] *Jeffersonian-Democrat* (Brookville, PA). "Reed Attack on Earle Challenged." Oct. 4, 1934.

[48] *Lebanon Daily News* (Lebanon, PA). "George Earle Gives Views on Austrian Revolt." July 26, 1934.

[49] Moffat, Jay Pierrepont letter to the Honorable George S. Messersmith, American Minister, Vienna, Austria, November 1, 1934.

[50] *Associated Press.* "Nationalism Leads Europeans to War." *Akron Beacon Journal.* July 27, 1934.

[51] Commonwealth of Pennsylvania, Department of Internal Affairs. *Industrial Statistics for Pennsylvania, 1916 to 1956.* Harrisburg, PA, 1959. 5.

[52] Beers, 118.

[53] Keller, 399.

[54] *Ibid.,* 401.

[55] Ibid., 402.

[56] Philadelphia Chamber of Commerce. "Legislative Bulletin, June 28, 1935." *Philadelphia Inquirer. March 17, 1935.*

[57] *United Press.* "What Earle Tells State." *News Herald* (Franklin, PA). Jan. 15. 1935.

[58] Beers, Paul D. *Pennsylvania Politics: Today and Yesterday.* University Park, PA: Penn State University Press, 1980. 122-123.

[59] *Time Magazine,* "Political Note: Labor Governor," July 5, 1937, 79.

[60] The Great Migration: A City Transformed (1916-1930). Oct. 10, 2017. https://greatmigrationphl.org.

[61] *Harrisburg Telegraph.* "Compromise Sought on Tax Measures to Meet Cost of Relief." May 1, 1935. 9.

[62] Pennsylvania Historical and Museum Commission. "Governor George Howard Earle III." Aug. 25, 2015. http://www.phmc.state.pa.us/portal/communities/governors/1876-1951/george-earle.html.

[63] *New York Times.* "Earle Hears Views on Bootleg Mining." Dec. 22, 1936. 28.

[64] *New York Times.* "New Deal on Coal Pledged by Earle." Dec. 24, 1936. 9.

[65] *New York Times.* "Coal Solution Evades Earle." April 17, 1938. 62.

[66] Davies, Lawrence E. "A Political Star Rises in Pennsylvania" *New York Times.* Nov. 29, 1936. 5.

[67] The Great Migration: A City Transformed (1916-1930). Oct. 10, 2017. https://greatmigrationphl.org.

[68] *New York Times.* "Editorial Comment on Governor Earle's Action." June 22, 1937.

[69] *United Press.* "Governor Earle Lifts Martial Law in Johnstown." *The Monongahela Daily Republican* (PA). June 24, 1937.

[70] *Life Magazine.* "Vigilantes Band as Nation Rings with Red Alarms." July 26, 1937.

[71] Davies, Lawrence E. "A Political Star Rises in Pennsylvania" *New York Times.* Nov. 29, 1936. 5.

[72] *Ibid.*

[73] *Ibid.*

[74] Beers, Paul D. *Pennsylvania Politics: Today and Yesterday*. University Park, PA: Penn State University Press, 1980. 130-131.

[75] *Ibid.*

[76] *Ibid.*, 135.

[77] Cummings, John M. "'Forgotten Man, Earle, Steps Down Gracefully." *Philadelphia Inquirer*, Jan. 7, 1939.

[78] Earle, George H. "Who Will Win the War?" *Philadelphia Inquirer*, Sept. 23, 1939.

[79] *Ibid.*

[80] *Evening News* (Harrisburg, PA). "'Maginot Line' 500 Miles at Sea Urged by Earle." Nov. 3, 1939. *International News Service.*

[81] *Associated Press.* "Earle Sees FDR on Foreign Post." *The Morning Call* (Allentown, PA). Jan. 24, 1940.

[82] *Los Angeles Times.* "New Envoy." Feb. 15, 1940.

[83] *Pittsburgh Post-Gazette.* "Bulgaria's King Boris Greets Diplomats." May 25, 1940.

[84] Colvin, Ian. *Chief of Intelligence.* London: Purnell & Sons, LTD, 1951.

[85] *International News Service.* "Earle Leaves for Bucharest." May 24, 1940.

[86] *Associated Press* (Istanbul). Nov. 13, 1940.

[87] ExplorePAHistory.com. "George H. Earle III Historical Marker." http://explorepahistory.com/hmarker.php?markerId=1-A-331.

[88] Earle, George H. cablegram to Secretary of State Cordell Hull, Sofia, Bulgaria, Nov. 21, 1940. In *Foreign Relations of the United States: Diplomatic Papers, 1940, General,* Vol. I. Document 165. Washington, DC: United States Government Printing Office, 1950.

[89] Earle, George H. cablegram to Secretary of State Cordell Hull, Sofia, Bulgaria, Dec. 18, 1940. In *Foreign Relations of the United States: Soviet Relations with Other Powers, 1940.* Document 189. Washington, DC: United States Government Printing Office, 1950.

[90] *United Press.* "A U.S. Diplomat Battles Nazis." Feb. 24, 1941.

[91] Padev, Michael. *Escape from the Balkans.* New York: Bobbs-Merrill Co., 1943. 153.

[92] Padev, 154.

[93] *Associated Press.* "Nazi Beaten by Earle, Envoy, Reported Dying." *Los Angeles Times.* Feb. 25, 1941. 1.

[94] Associated Press, "Cambria Judges Wire Earle Congratulations," *The Philadelphia Inquirer*, February 25, 1941, p. 1.

[95] Hadley, Harold. "Adventures of a Diplomat." *Philadelphia Daily News.* Jan. 28, 1963. 5.

[96] *United Press.* "Nazi Industrialist Admits He Was Man Earle Struck." *Morning Call* (Allentown, PA). Feb. 28, 1941. 1.

[97] *Shamokin News-Dispatch* (Shamokin, PA). "U.S. Envoy to Bulgaria 'Always Craved Excitement,' Says Wife." Feb. 24, 1941. 12.

[98] *Ibid.*

[99] Padev, 43.

[100] *The Daily Independent (*Murphysboro, IL). "Wild Bill Donovan has a Look in Bulgaria." March 3, 1941. 6.

[101] *Associated Press.* "Earle's Detention at Bulgarian Line Stirs U.S. Protest." *Philadelphia Inquirer.* March 3, 1941. 1.

[102] Kluckhohn, Frank L. "Hull Gives Notice: Freezing of Bulgaria's Credit Awaits Formal News of Occupation." *New York Times.* March 1, 1941.

[103] *Associated Press.* "George Earle Bested Nazis." *Poughkeepsie Eagle News* (NY). Feb. 11, 1942. 5.

[104] Hadley, Harold. "Adventures of a Diplomat." *Philadelphia Daily News*. Jan 29, 1963. 17.

[105] Hadley, Harold. "Adventures of a Diplomat." *Philadelphia Daily News*. Jan 29, 1963. 20.

[106] *Ibid.*

[107] Farago, Ladislas. *The Game of Foxes.* New York: David McKay & Co, 1971. 573.

[108] *Philadelphia Inquirer.* "Earle Returns, Escaped Death Twice." Jan. 30, 1942. 1.

[109] Office of the Chief of Naval Operations Naval History Division. *Dictionary of American Naval Fighting Ships.* DANFS: USS Hermitage (AP-54). https://www.ibiblio.org/hyperwar/USN/ships/danfs/AP/ap54.html.

[110] National Personnel Records Center. "Service Record of Veteran: EARLE, George Howard, Request Number: 2-20558304190." *National Archives and Records Administration.* July 25, 2017.

[111] Roosevelt, Franklin D. Memorandum for Mr. Shipman, Washington, DC, Dec. 18, 1942. FDR Presidential Library, Poughkeepsie, NY. http://www.fdrlibrary.marist.edu/_resources/images/psf/psf000334.pdf.

[112] National Personnel Records Center. "Service Record of Veteran: EARLE, George Howard, Request Number: 2-20558304190." *National Archives and Records Administration.* July 25, 2017.

[113] Farago, Ladislas. *The Game of Foxes.* New York: David McKay & Co, 1971. 574.

[114] Baldwin, Hanson W. *Great Mistakes of the War.* New York: Harper & Brothers, 1950. 14.

[115] Liddell Hart, B.H. *The German Generals Talk.* New York: William Morrow & Co., 1948. 292-293.

[116] Fowler, George. "Could Roosevelt Have Ended World War II Earlier." *Human Events.* April 20, 1985.

[117] Deringill, Selim. *Turkish Foreign Policy During the Second World War.* Cambridge: Cambridge University Press, 1991. 118.

[118] Hull, Cordell. Telegram to American Embassy, Ankara. Jan. 13, 1942. National Archives and Records Administration.

[119] Farago, Ladislas. *The Game of Foxes.* New York: David McKay & Co, 1971. 572.

[120] Farago, 575.

[121] Farago, 334.

[122] UK Archives. "Secret" MI5 Name Trace Request Re: Louis Matzhold. Feb. 9, 1940.

[123] Farago, 576.

[124] Kross, Peter. "Creating the OSS: FDR's Network of Personal Spies." Warfare History Network, Aug. 19, 2015. https://warfarehistorynetwork.com/2015/08/21/creating-the-oss-fdrs-network-of-personal-spies/.

[125] Harrison, Leland. Cablegram to Secretary of State Cordell Hull, Berne, Switzerland. Feb. 2, 1943. National Archives and Records Administration.

[126] Triantafyllopoulos, Christos. "Allen Dulles and the Compromise of OSS Codes in WWII." *Christos Military and Intelligence Corner.* May 23, 2012. https:// chris-intel-corner.blogspot.com/ 2012 / 05 / allen-dulles-and-compromise-of-oss.html.

[127] Colvin, Ian. *Master Spy.* New York: McGraw-Hill Book Company, Inc. 1951. 165-166.

[128] Farago, 577, 581.

[129] Farago, 577-578.

[130] Farago, 578.

[131] Farago, 578-579.

[132] Military Intelligence Service. "Italian Air Attaché Report." April 5, 1944. National Archives and Records Administration.

[133] Farago, Ladislas. *The Game of Foxes.* New York: David McKay & Co, 1971. 570 - 581.

[134] Dulles, Allen. *Germany's Underground: The Anti-Nazi Resistance.* New York: Macmillan, 1947. 136.

[135] Admiral Wilhelm Canaris, Chief of the *Abwehr.* Source: Bundesarchiv, Bild 146-1979-013-43 / CC-BY-SA 3.0, CC BY-SA 3.0 de.

[136] Franz von Papen, German Ambassador to Turkey, Last Chancellor before Hitler.
Source: Bundesarchiv, Bild 183-1988-0113-500 / CC-BY-SA 3.0.

[137] Farago, 6-9.

[138] Farago, 6.

[139] Höhne, Heinz. *Canaris: Hitler's Master Spy.* Garden City, New York: Doubleday & Co.,1979. 482.

[140] Höhne, 483.

[141] Fowler.

[142] Leverkuehn, Paul. *German Military Intelligence.* New York: Praeger Inc., 1954. 25, 206.

[143] Paine, Lauran. *German Military Intelligence in World War II: The Abwehr.* New York: Stein and Day, 1984. 29.

[144] Von Papen, Fritz. *Memoirs.* New York: E.P. Dutton & Co., 1953. 499.

[145] Sykes, Christopher. *Tormented Loyalty.* New York: Harper and Row, 1969.

[146] Von Klemperer, Klemens. *German Resistance Against Hitler: The Search for Allies Abroad, 1938-1945.* Oxford: Clarendon Press, 1992. 328.

[147] Von Papen, Franz. *Memoirs.* New York: E.P. Dutton & Co., 1953. 499.

[148] Earle, George H. "FDR's Tragic Mistake." *Confidential*, Aug. 1958. 58.

[149] Hoffman, Peter. *The History of the German Resistance, 1939-1945.* Cambridge, MA: MIT Press, 1977. 276-277.

[150] Von Klemperer, 329.

[151] "Exposé on the Readiness of a Powerful German Group to Prepare and Assist Allied Military Operations Against Nazi Germany." Record Group 226, Entry 180, A 3304, Roll 68. National Archives and Records Administration.

[152] Balfour, Michael and Julian Frisby. *Helmuth von Moltke: A Leader Against Hitler.* London: MacMillan, 1972. 269-277.

[153] Höhne, 484.

[154] Balfour and Frisby, 278.

[155] Balfour and Frisby, 278.

[156] Earle, George H. III and George Fowler. "Roosevelt's Fatal Error." *Human Events.* March 24, 1960.

[157] "TOP SECRET DATA RE EARLE CASE" File. FDR Presidential Library, White House Naval Aide File, PSF Earle, George H., Subject File E, Box 146. National Archives and Records Administration.

[158] Hoover Institution Archives, Albert C. Wedemeyer Collection, Box 35, Folder 22.

[159] Lawrence W. Earle, interview by author, Bryn Mawr, PA, Dec. 4, 2016.

[160] Persico, 270.

[161] Persico, 382 -384.

[162] Earle, George H. cablegram to Harry Hopkins, Istanbul, Turkey, Sept. 13, 1943. FDR Presidential Library, White House Naval Aide File, PSF Earle, George H., Subject File E, Box 146. National Archives and Records Administration.

[163] Earle, George H. letter to President Franklin D. Roosevelt, Istanbul, Turkey, Oct. 1, 1943. FDR Presidential Library, White House Naval Aide File, PSF Earle,

George H., Subject File E, Box 146. National Archives and Records Administration.

[164] Leahy, William to President Franklin D. Roosevelt, May 26, 1944. FDR Presidential Library, White House Naval Aide File, PSF Earle, George H., Subject File E, Box 146. National Archives and Records Administration.

[165] Earle, George H. message to President Franklin D. Roosevelt, Istanbul, Turkey, April. 13, 1944. FDR Presidential Library, White House Naval Aide File, PSF Earle, George H., Subject File E, Box 146. National Archives and Records Administration.

[166] Earle, George H. cablegram to President Franklin D. Roosevelt, Istanbul, Turkey, April. 17, 1944. FDR Presidential Library, White House Naval Aide File, PSF Earle, George H., Subject File E, Box 146. National Archives and Records Administration.

[167] Earle, George H. letter to Admiral Wilson Brown, Istanbul, Turkey, July. 8, 1944. FDR Presidential Library, White House Naval Aide File, PSF Earle, George H., Subject File E, Box 146. National Archives and Records Administration.

[168] Earle, George H. letter to Admiral William D. Leahy, Istanbul, Turkey, Aug. 16, 1944. FDR Presidential Library, White House Naval Aide File, PSF Earle, George H., Subject File E, Box 146. National Archives and Records Administration.

[169] Earle, George H. report to Admiral Wilson Brown, Istanbul, Turkey, Aug. 16, 1944. FDR Presidential Library, White House Naval Aide File, PSF Earle, George H., Subject File E, Box 146. National Archives and Records Administration.

[170] Country Studies: Romania. "Armistice Negotiations and Soviet Occupation." Chapter 23, Library of Congress. http://countrystudies.us/romania/23.htm

[171] Earle, George H. letter to President Franklin D. Roosevelt, Istanbul, Turkey, Aug. 22, 1944. FDR Presidential Library, White House Naval Aide File, PSF Earle, George H., Subject File E, Box 146. National Archives and Records Administration.

[172] Bergery, Gaston. Attachment to Earle's letter. Istanbul, Turkey. FDR Presidential Library, White House Naval Aide File, PSF Earle, George H., Subject File E, Box 146. National Archives and Records Administration.

[173] Earle, George H. letter to Admiral Wilson Brown, Istanbul, Turkey, Sept. 3, 1944. FDR Presidential Library, White House Naval Aide File, PSF Earle, George H., Subject File E, Box 146. National Archives and Records Administration.

[174] Earle, George H. letter to President Franklin D. Roosevelt, Istanbul, Turkey, Oct. 31, 1944. FDR Presidential Library, White House Naval Aide File, PSF Earle, George H., Subject File E, Box 146. National Archives and Records Administration.

[175] Earle, George H. letter to President Franklin D. Roosevelt, Istanbul, Turkey, Dec. 9, 1944. FDR Presidential Library, White House Naval Aide File, PSF Earle, George H., Subject File E, Box 146. National Archives and Records Administration.

[176] West, Diana. *American Betrayal*. New York: St. Martin's Press, 2013. 210.

[177] "TOP SECRET DATA RE EARLE CASE" File. FDR Presidential Library, White House Naval Aide File, PSF Earle, George H., Subject File E, Box 146. National Archives and Records Administration.

[178] Earle, George H. "FDR's Tragic Mistake." *Confidential*, Aug. 1958. 58.

[179] Fischer, Benjamin B. "The Katyn Controversy: Stalin's Killing Field." *Studies in Intelligence*, 1999. 64.

[180] *The Katyn Forest Massacre: Hearings Before the Select Committee to Conduct an Investigation of the Facts, Evidence and Circumstances of the Katyn Forest Massacre*. 82nd Cong., 2204. (Statement of George H. Earle).

[181] National Personnel Records Center. "Service Record of Veteran: EARLE, George Howard, Request Number: 2-20558304190." *National Archives and Records Administration*. July 25, 2017.

[182] Earle, George H. letter to Anna Boettiger, Philadelphia, PA, March 21, 1945. FDR Presidential Library, White House Naval Aide File, PSF Earle, George H., Subject File E, Box 146. National Archives and Records Administration.

[183] Boettiger, Anna note to Grace Tully, Washington, DC, n.d. FDR Presidential Library, White House Naval Aide File, PSF Earle, George H., Subject File E, Box 146. National Archives and Records Administration.

[184] Roosevelt, Franklin D. Letter to Commander George H. Earle III. "March 24, 1945 Letter from President Franklin D. Roosevelt." *George Howard Earle Papers.* Philadelphia, PA: The Historical Society of Pennsylvania.

[185] Earle, George H. letter to President Franklin D. Roosevelt, Philadelphia, PA, March 26, 1945. FDR Presidential Library, White House Naval Aide File, PSF Earle, George H., Subject File E, Box 146. National Archives and Records Administration.

[186] Roosevelt, Franklin D. letter to George H. Earle, March 29, 1945. FDR Presidential Library, White House Naval Aide File, PSF Earle, George H., Subject File E, Box 146. National Archives and Records Administration.

[187] Earle, George H. letter to U.S. Navy Bureau of Personnel, Samoa, Oct. 1945. FDR Presidential Library, White House Naval Aide File, PSF Earle, George H., Subject File E, Box 146. National Archives and Records Administration.

[188] Earle, George H. letter to U.S. Navy Bureau of Personnel, Samoa, Oct. 1945. FDR Presidential Library, White House Naval Aide File, PSF Earle, George H., Subject File E, Box 146. National Archives and Records Administration.

[189] National Personnel Records Center. "Service Record of Veteran: EARLE, George Howard, Request Number: 2-20558304190." *National Archives and Records Administration.* July 25, 2017.

[190] National Personnel Records Center, "Service Record of Veteran: EARLE, George Howard, Request Number: 2-20558304190," *National Archives and Records Administration*, July 25, 2017.

[191] *New York Times.* "Earle Offers Russia Atomic Ultimatum." March 23, 1946.

[192] *Philadelphia Inquirer.* "Papen Offered to Betray Hitler, Earle Asserts in Defending Intercession." Jan. 30, 1949. 31.

[193] *Muncie Evening Press* (Muncie, IN). Nov.15, 1952. 4.

[194] Goldstein, Robert Justin. "Prelude to McCarthyism: The Making of a Blacklist." *Prologue Magazine*, Fall 2006, Vol. 38, No. 3. National Archives and Records Administration. https://www.archives.gov/publications/prologue/2006/fall/agloso.html

[195] *Associated Press.* "Russia Dreams of World Domination, Former Diplomat George Earle Warns Congressmen." March 29, 1947.

[196] Hummel, Jeffrey Rogers. "Operation Keelhaul—Exposed" *Reason* (1974). San Jose State University Scholarly Works. 4-9. https://scholarworks.sjsu.edu/cgi/viewcontent.cgi?article=1017&context=econ_pub.

[197] *Associated Press.* "Russia Dreams of World Domination, Former Diplomat George Earle Warns Congressmen." March 29, 1947.

[198] *New York Times.* "Truman Answers Earle: Says He Has No Fear of Communists Taking Over Government." April 4, 1947.

[199] *Neosho Daily News* (MO). "Rulers of Russia Called Murderers by George Earle." April 29, 1947.

[200] Peterman, Ivan. "Vishinsky Says U.S. Plots Atomic War on Russia in Drive to Conquer World." *Philadelphia Inquirer.* Sept. 19, 1947. 1.

[201] *Corpus Christi Caller-Times* (TX). "Sandburg Labels George H. Earle a Warmonger." October 6, 1947.

[202] *United States Foreign Policy for a Postwar Recovery Program, Before the House of Representatives Committee on Foreign Affairs,* 80th Cong. 1224 *et seq* (Feb. 12, 1948) (testimony of George H. Earle III, Governor of the Commonwealth of Pennsylvania).

[203] *United States Foreign Policy for a Postwar Recovery Program, Before the House of Representatives Committee on Foreign Affairs,* 80th Cong. 1224 *et seq* (Feb. 12, 1948) (testimony of George H. Earle III, Governor of the Commonwealth of Pennsylvania).

[204] *United States Foreign Policy for a Postwar Recovery Program, Before the House of Representatives Committee on Foreign Affairs,* 80th Cong. 1224 *et seq* (Feb. 12, 1948) (testimony of George H. Earle III, Governor of the Commonwealth of Pennsylvania).

[205] *United States Foreign Policy for a Postwar Recovery Program, Before the House of Representatives Committee on Foreign Affairs,* 80th Cong. 1224 *et seq* (Feb. 12, 1948) (testimony of George H. Earle III, Governor of the Commonwealth of Pennsylvania).

[206] *United States Foreign Policy for a Postwar Recovery Program, Before the House of Representatives Committee on Foreign Affairs,* 80th Cong. 1224 *et seq* (Feb. 12, 1948) (testimony of George H. Earle III, Governor of the Commonwealth of Pennsylvania).

[207] Cummings, John M. "Presidential Unconcern About the Commie Peril." *Philadelphia Inquirer*, Sept. 28, 1948. 20.

[208] *The Katyn Forest Massacre: Hearings Before the United States House of Representatives Select Committee to Conduct an Investigation of the Facts, Evidence and Circumstances of the Katyn Forest Massacre.* 82nd Cong., 2196 *et seq.* (Testimony of George H. Earle III). https://archive.org/stream/katynforestmassa07unit/katynforestmassa07unit_djvu.txt.

[209] *The Katyn Forest Massacre: Hearings Before the United States House of Representatives Select Committee to Conduct an Investigation of the Facts, Evidence and Circumstances of the Katyn Forest Massacre.* 82nd Cong., 2196 *et seq.* (Statement of George H. Earle III). https://archive.org/stream/katynforestmassa07unit/katynforestmassa07unit_djvu.txt.

[210] *The Katyn Forest Massacre: Hearings Before the United States House of Representatives Select Committee to Conduct an Investigation of the Facts, Evidence and Circumstances of the Katyn Forest Massacre.* 82nd Cong., 2196 *et seq.* (Statement of George H. Earle III). https://archive.org/stream/katynforestmassa07unit/katynforestmassa07unit_djvu.txt.

[211] Earle, George H. letter to U.S. Army General Albert C. Wedemeyer, Radnor, PA, Nov. 7, 1958. Albert C. Wedemeyer Papers, [Box 35, Folder 22], Hoover Institution Archives.

[212] Earle, George H. letter to U.S. Army General Albert C. Wedemeyer, Radnor, PA, Nov. 1958. Albert C. Wedemeyer Papers, [Box 35, Folder 22], Hoover Institution Archives.

[213] Earle, George H. letter to U.S. Army General Albert C. Wedemeyer, Radnor, PA, Dec. 11, 1958. Albert C. Wedemeyer Papers, [Box 35, Folder 22], Hoover Institution Archives.

[214] Lordan, Francis M. "George H. Earle 3d, Governor, Soldier, Sportsman, Dies." *Philadelphia Inquirer.* Dec. 31, 1974. 1.

[215] The National Archives of the UK, MI5 Security Files, Subject: Molnar, Adrienne.

Index

CPSIA information can be obtained
at www.ICGtesting.com
Printed in the USA
BVHW041148201221
624513BV00015B/415